Children of Faith

Islamic Strategies for Raising Mentally Strong and Emotionally Balanced Kids

SARAH GULFRAZ

Copyright © 2025 Sarah Gulfraz

Sarah Gulfraz has asserted her right to be identified as the author of this Work in accordance with the Copyright, Designs and Patents Act 1988.

All rights reserved.

No portion of this book may be reproduced in any form, stored in a retrieval system, stored in a database, or published/transmitted in any form or by any means, electronic, mechanical, photocopying, recording or otherwise, without prior written permission of the publisher.

Dedication

~ Bismillah ~

May Allah (swt) accept our efforts and grant us success in this life and the next. Ameen.

In dedication to my loving family and all their support.

Contents

1. Introduction — 1
2. Introduction to Islamic Parenting — 5
3. Building a Strong Foundation of Faith — 20
4. Encouraging Emotional Intelligence and Resilience — 33
5. Effective Communication and Listening — 50
6. Discipline with Compassion and Fairness — 58
7. Building Self-Esteem and Confidence — 67
8. Teaching Gratitude and Contentment — 77
9. Encouraging Healthy Relationships and Social Skills — 85
10. Managing Stress and Mental Health — 95
11. Role of Parents & Community in Supporting Children's Development — 101
12. Conclusion — 108

Find Out More — 112

Chapter One

Introduction

Families are vital social entities that collectively shape society. Harmonious families will positively influence society, whereas society cannot progress if families become morally deficient. From birth, every individual learns their first lessons about home, family members, and society within their family.

To improve society, we must enhance the quality of families and concentrate on raising children in a constructive manner. Prophet Muhammad (PBUH), according to a story ascribed to Hazrat Aisha (RA), stated:

> *"The best among you are those who are best to their families, and I am the best among you to my family."*
> *(Tirmidhi)*

The process of encouraging and nurturing a child's intellectual, social, emotional, and physical growth from birth to adulthood is known as parenting. The child's soul is like an uncut, priceless gem that Allah (SWT) has entrusted to our protection as parents. The task of transforming that priceless gem into a stunning shape that pleases Allah (SWT) is an incredible duty. Making sure our child develops into a decent and moral adult is our sacred responsibility as Muslims. The unity of Islamic existence is another manifestation of Allah's (SWT) oneness (Tawhid). To Islamic global civilisation, we must raise our children to be morally upright individuals.

As adherents of Islam, a religious tradition revealed by Allah (SWT), we recognise that all of these areas of support and promotion must occur within the bounds of the Quran's teachings and the Prophet Muhammad's (PBUH) guidance. To be regarded as a parent, whether a mother or a father, one must rise to the occasion and make sure that all facets of their children's lives—both the material and the spiritual realms—have been nurtured and maintained to the best of their parents' abilities.

For parents, children are both a gift and a responsibility, or Amanah. It's our responsibility to ensure that they develop into diligent, fruitful, and—above all—godly people who will benefit them and the Ummah as well. A child's excellent upbringing is the best gift his parents can give them. Every parent aspires to raise a morally upright child. Which parent wouldn't overflow with gladness when blessed with a devout child who fills their eyes and hearts with much comfort and joy?

Because Allah (SWT) bestows kindness via them, such a child benefits the parents both here on Earth and in the Hereafter. However, with so many effective parenting theories, it can seem intimidating and perplexing. It's understandable why most parents struggle to raise devout and productive kids! This book simplified the fundamentals of Islamic parenting to make it easier for parents. These will direct and help you to become productive parents raising productive kids if you follow through on them.

Everyone experiences both good and bad things. But these experiences are all confined within the boundaries of the home. Only families teach people of all genders the value of alleviating family members' pain and allowing them to completely enjoy their blessings. Thus, it's essential to raise kids in a favourable way to have a healthy family and, in turn, a healthy society.

Parents must prepare children at home during their formative years to prepare them for a better life. A person's personality that develops throughout this time gets firmly established. Parents need to understand that it's difficult to make up for mistakes made during this stage of their child's development later on. It's uncommon for such experiences to result in a positive revolution in a person, although corrective actions can be feasible in extraordinary situations involving startling events that could mark a turning point in his life. As a result, it's essential to give the child's early years a loving and well-rounded upbringing.

Children need to learn from their parents about Allah's (SWT) creation plan and how the world is a test for humanity. While one type of life can bring people to Paradise, another renders them worthy of eternal exile. A person's domestic and external concerns are connected to this trying aspect of life. This issue's crux is that people should prioritise their Creator above all else. When Allah's (SWT) backing is severed, a person who makes other things their first priority will fail the test and end up penniless in the Hereafter.

Muslim parents ought to make an effort to provide their kids with a solid foundation of monotheism and Islamic principles. Worship and devotion to Allah (SWT) should become essential aspects of their character. They should observe fasting and prayers. They should be inspired to do good deeds and charity and become passionate about studying the Quran and Hadith every day. Knowing this, parents need to teach their kids duty-consciousness instead of right-consciousness. Children who are raised this way will behave as models of the highest moral standards and advance society.

Parenting is not about setting aside particular times to sit with children and give them advice or lectures. Giving the kids a choice between the correct and wrong courses in real-world situations at home guarantees that they will be raised properly. In these situations, family members must receive the proper instruction, emotions must be managed, and personal losses must be suffered. It's necessary to steer their thoughts in the proper path. These conditions are used to provide upbringing rather than giving sermons.

If parents rear their children carelessly without clear parenting norms, it's impossible to provide them with a solid education, especially in a Muslim family. In this age of globalisation, parenting knowledge is, therefore, one of the things that must be learnt and put into practice as the cornerstone of childrearing. Parenting abilities lead to effective teaching, nurturing, and leading, all crucial in defining a family's overall health.

Developing a realistic mindset and a spirit of action in children is the best way to ensure their success. Children should have their inner potential awakened, their circumstances understood, and their lives shaped appropriately. Genuine development is not granted by others; it's the result of devotion and hard work. This is the way to go for those who care about their children's education and upbringing.

This book provides parents with helpful advice on raising emotionally and intellectually resilient kids using Islamic values. Every chapter provides practical advice and insights into different facets of parenting, assisting in the establishment of a loving and encouraging atmosphere that fosters children's spiritual and emotional development.

Every parent and guardian will use this book as a guide to nurturing their children properly. It has great ideas for laying solid national foundations as well as important guidelines for personal preparation. Adopting the whole and comprehensive Islamic method of rearing and reforming is the only option. May Allah (SWT) encourage Muslims to make Islam their guiding principle in their beliefs and creeds, to make it their real objective and refuge in their actions and education, and to adopt it as their ideal for achieving Islamic unity.

Chapter Two

Introduction to Islamic Parenting

Principles of Islamic Parenting

A child has an inherent and natural right to be raised and cared for by their parent. Additionally, it's the parent's responsibility to raise and care for their child. Parenthood is an identity that describes a person's relationship of caregiving to a child and has aspects determined by biological and social factors. According to this definition of parenthood, parents and children have complementary, reciprocal, and interdependent rights and responsibilities.

Many people may believe that being a parent only entails having kids. However, being a parent is a long-lasting and challenging journey in which one not only brings a new human life into the world but also guides them towards adulthood. It's a parent's responsibility to take a physically and emotionally reliant child and nurture and raise them into a fully self-sufficient adult.

Being a parent means acknowledging that you bear the primary responsibility for your child's education, safety, well-being, emotional development, and eventual achievement of adulthood.

As parents, it can be difficult to instil fundamental Islamic principles in your kids, particularly if you live in a non-Muslim nation. How do you get them to balance the afterlife with the Dunya? How do you get them to focus on learning about Islam?

Getting your fundamentals right is the first step. Your child shouldn't be exposed to Islam "later on in their life." The best gift you can give your child as a parent is to raise them well from the beginning of their life. Allah (SWT) has given us children as an Amanah. They are a wonderful gift, but they also come with a greater duty. Our responsibility is to bring them up to be morally upright, pious, and dedicated people.

First of all, priority should be given to the role of intention and responsibility because these are crucial components of all actions, including parenting. Approach child-rearing as a divine duty, shaping future generations who will contribute meaningfully to the ummah (Muslim community).

> *The Prophet Muhammad (PBUH) emphasised that "actions are judged by intentions." (Sahih Bukhari)*

Their upbringing determines a child's destiny and how they develop into a perfect, responsible, and authentic Muslim adult. The goal should be to bring up children to be decent Muslims and decent people in general. If, as parents, you can raise your child properly, you have achieved the world's most valuable reward.

Every child is seen to be innocent and devout at birth, and what he eventually learns from his surroundings—including what he observes, absorbs, feels, and hears from others—matters. All children are blameless and lack the innate characteristics needed to behave rebelliously or mischievously.

Young children always develop their sense of right and wrong and appropriate behaviour in their surroundings. For children to continue doing what is right and pure, it's the parent's duty to teach them how to accomplish this, choose their surroundings, and choose the kind of people to surround themselves with. This indicates that even if your kids make mistakes, they are innocent.

Thus, handle them with care. Instead of reprimanding them straight away if they make a mistake, attempt to find out why they did it. Their surroundings or influence may be the source of the issue. While showing affection is vital, know when and where to draw the line. Though they're not flawless, children are pure. As they develop into responsible adults, they will inevitably make mistakes.

Rules and regulations are necessary for any entity. Since the family unit is an institution, it requires laws to function properly; otherwise, anarchy will result. Your family can remain organised by adhering to rules such as having a set bedtime, tidying their rooms daily, brushing their teeth before bed, waking for Fajr prayer, eating with their right hand, and saying "Assalamu alaikum" before entering a room

Giving your child tiny tasks to accomplish from an early age may help them develop a sense of responsibility. For instance, they may take their plates to the kitchen after eating or put away their toys after playing. This will instil an early sense of responsibility in them.

> *"Every one of you is a guardian and is responsible for his charges. The ruler who has authority over people, is a guardian and is responsible for them; a man is a guardian of his family and is responsible for them; a woman is a guardian of her husband's house and children and is responsible for them; a slave is a guardian of his master's property and is responsible for it; so all of you are guardians and are responsible for your charges." (Sahih Bukhari)*

Since he or she is fresh to the world, the child is unsure what to do. Who is good by nature, but it needs to be cultivated. Leading, guiding, and caring for them falls on his parents. Raising self-sufficient, accountable individuals who will contribute positively to society is the basic aim of parenting.

The most crucial thing is to always pray for your children, asking Allah (SWT), who provides guidance, Ar Rashid, to lead them in the correct direction and help you make the greatest choices for them.

Understanding the Stages of Parenting in Islamic Teachings

To raise our children, Islamic scholars stress that there are three stages of parenting, and each one calls for a distinct strategy and mode of instruction.

> *The Prophet Muhammad (PBUH) said: "Play with them for the first seven years (of their life); then teach them for the next seven years; then advise them for the next seven years (and after that)." (Sunah Abu Dawood)*

We can categorise a child's upbringing into three stages based on the Hadith of the Prophet (PBUH) mentioned above.

The First Stage: Age 0-7 (Love and Mercy)

While allowing our children to play, we must also be proactive as parents to cultivate a close bond with them. During these formative years, children are continuously impacted by their environment and acquire knowledge through observation. More than anyone else, children imitate their parents. The Prophet Muhammad (PBUH) showed great compassion for children and urged parents to do likewise.

> *"He is not of us who does not have mercy on young children, nor honour the elderly." (Sunah Abu Dawood)*

The foundation years are the starting point for the relationship with them. If this is a firm foundation, the following years will be considerably simpler. Poor foundation formation will make the upcoming years more difficult. Also, it's important to start gently introducing the concept of Allah (SWT) and the life of the Holy Prophet (PBUH) through basic Islamic teachings and stories to nurture faith in them.

The Second Stage: Age 7-14 (Discipline and Training)

Children are prepared for Islamic ethics and logical reasoning when they turn seven. Children are like sponges at this age and are prepared to absorb whatever you show, teach, and say. Teaching kids secular and religious information, halal vs haram, and everything else they need to know is the second stage of rearing. The main goals of parenting should be to instil discipline, accountability, and healthy habits.

> *"Instruct your children to pray when they are seven years old, and (gently) discipline them for it when they are ten." (Sunan Abu Dawood)*

Children are still developing their sense of right and wrong. For children to continue making choices that benefit them, it's the parents' responsibility to teach them appropriate behaviour, how to select their surroundings, and the type of people they surround themselves with.

Similarly, kids require a set of rules to govern their conduct, allowing them the flexibility to act as they like. They won't understand what is and isn't appropriate if they don't know the boundaries. Society would be in disarray if there were no boundaries. Children will have the parameters to act within the boundaries and won't be left wondering and perplexed if they're taught in advance what appropriate and excellent behaviour is.

As a parent, establish guidelines and limits for all family members, including yourself, and make sure your children understand why they must follow them. As you gently explain, allow them to ask questions since they appreciate logical reasoning. Emphasis should be placed on teaching morality and ethics, such as kindness, honesty, respect, and the effects of one's conduct.

The Third Stage: Age 14-21 (Friendship and Mentorship)

At this period, relationships built on trust and friendship are formed, and children become independent and form their own personalities after reaching 14 (also known as puberty). Parents should mentor them without being overbearing, focus on deep conversations, and advise them gently to keep them on the right path. Simply put, during these important years, befriend them, guide them, and try your hardest. Remember that they're now fully grown adults, and according to Islamic teachings, it's their responsibility to determine what is right or wrong.

The Importance of Nurturing Mental and Emotional Well-being in Children

A vital component of our general health and well-being is our mental health. Supporting your child's mental health is a major responsibility of yours as a parent. A solid foundation is created by providing your child with loving and nurturing care, which aids in developing the cognitive and emotional abilities necessary for a happy, healthy, and full life.

Indeed, children, teenagers, and their families deal with a lot of stress and various issues linked to mental health. Fortunately, there are strategies to support mental well-being in challenging circumstances. In fact, strong resources are available to parents and other caregivers that can assist children in developing resilience and thriving in any situation.

Children learn the skills necessary to control their feelings, solve problems, communicate, and form strong bonds through positive experiences and secure, long-lasting relationships. Healthy mental and emotional growth is acquiring these and other vital abilities. Children's emotional health is just as vital as their physical health is. Their development is incomplete when their social and emotional needs are neglected.

Taking care of children's mental health and rights are significant and essential components of Islam. Every child deserves to be loved, cared for, and guided. They are entitled to intellectual and spiritual instruction as well as chances to develop into morally upright and kind people.

Therefore, it's essential that we raise our kids in ways that support their healthy development and enable them to face obstacles in life. The Prophet Muhammad (PBUH) was known for his tenderness toward children. He emphasised showing love to them as an essential part of raising them properly.

> *Anas ibn Malik (RA) reported: "I never saw anyone who was more compassionate towards children than the Messenger of Allah (PBUH)." (Sahih Muslim)*

The way we treat and care for our children greatly impacts many facets of their lives, particularly their mental health and general wellness. We empower our children when we support their mental and emotional health, which enables them to overcome obstacles, accomplish their goals, and provide the same support to others. It's our duty as a community to protect this right by making sure our kids feel heard and safe.

Providing Spiritual and Faith-Based Care

Improving our general mental health is facilitated by effectively connecting with Allah (SWT). Particularly, a number of verses in the Quran emphasise how having faith can help us cope with stress and adversity.

> *"Those who believe and their hearts are assured by the remembrance of Allah, Certainly in the Remembrance of Allah do the hearts find peace." (Quran 13:28)*

Moreover, children who grow up with faith learn to always rely on Allah (SWT) during hardships. This strengthens their ability to handle challenges and setbacks calmly. In turn, fostering a love of faith in our kids significantly impacts their mental and emotional health, especially when done early.

Prayer and supplications are integral to daily life for Muslims and other societies with deep religious roots. Our responsibility is to carefully and patiently teach our children these traditions so that they can have a solid relationship with Allah (SWT) throughout their lives.

By presenting Allah (SWT) in this tender and caring manner, we enable our children to learn about an All-caring Creator who they can rely on for support and guidance in any circumstance.

Nurturing Through Morality and Goodness

Children's perceptions of the world are positively influenced when we love them and set a good example. By providing our children with a role model who teaches patience, selflessness, and respect through love and care, particularly from an early age, we enable them to naturally develop these sentiments towards their environment and its people.

> *"When Allah wills good for a household, He instills kindness among them"* (Musnad Ahmad)

This hadith emphasises how crucial it is to create a loving and caring atmosphere in the home to help kids develop good character.

Given that life is full of ups and downs, we must educate our kids on resilience in ways that will increase their sense of confidence and self-worth. Congratulate them on their efforts to pursue their interests and education and motivate them to keep going for their objectives. If they're having trouble getting back on their feet, assist them in developing coping mechanisms that will make these difficulties simpler to deal with in the future.

> *"And whoever relies upon Allah – then He is sufficient for him. Indeed, Allah will accomplish His purpose. Allah has already set for everything a [decreed] extent"* (Quran 65:3)

Teaching children to rely on Allah and have patience in hardships strengthens their resilience.

Children must hear and feel their family and community's affection for them. They can bounce back from any setback in life because they know they have a network of people to look up to and are free to make errors.

> After all, the Quran tells us: *"For indeed, with [every] hardship, there is relief. Indeed, with [every] hardship, there is relief."* (Quran 94:5-6)

Therefore, we should model goodness for our kids and foster their mental and emotional health to help them realise this.

Each child's optimal growth and well-being depend heavily on their mental health. In addition to being able to handle difficulties and adjust to change, children in good mental health are also more likely to feel good about themselves, form positive relationships with others, and enjoy life.

It's our responsibility as a community to support our children on their journey towards mental health, which includes positively fostering their emotional and mental welfare.

Nurturing in the Community and Nature

Connecting with our environment and those around us facilitates maintaining a sense of groundedness and presence in our relationships and mental health. In a world where technology permeates every aspect of our lives, it can be challenging to keep our kids and ourselves away from screens for extended periods as we worry that we might be missing out on the world around us.

However, not always being linked to our digital environments is good. As a family, spend time exploring the area and learning about the local people and environment. Encourage your kids to engage with other kids through team sports or playgroups and to play outside. If you do this, your children will feel more confident, have better physical health, and be inspired to express themselves. Additionally, it fosters their empathy and teaches children how to share and assist others.

> *"The most beloved people to Allah are those who are most beneficial to people." (Al-Mujam al-Awsaṭ)*

Teaching children to engage with their community and help others fosters a sense of belonging and social responsibility. Humans are naturally social beings, and Allah (SWT) is pleased when we bring joy to His creations.

> *"And cooperate in righteousness and piety, but do not cooperate in sin and aggression" (Quran 5:2)*

When we come together in kindness, we're rewarded with a happy environment and advantages for our mental and emotional health. We build a strong support system that we can rely on in times of need by interacting with one another as a community and the things around us.

Objectives of Raising Mentally and Emotionally Strong Children

Parenting goals are particular targets or objectives that parents set to direct their approach to developing emotionally and cognitively strong children. These objectives act as a road map, giving parents direction and purpose as they traverse the challenging process of raising children. They cover a range of facets of a child's growth, including cognitive, social, emotional, and physical development.

Children have exceptional cognitive abilities in various areas during the first four years of life, including language, reasoning, and social cognition. These early cognitive accomplishments are most noticeable in the social domain. Infants prefer social to non-social stimuli from an early age, are influenced by other people's attention and behaviour as they see and encode the world, and develop complex expectations of other people's behaviour.

By the time they are four years old, children have a complex understanding of themselves and other people. They can reason about intangible, abstract ideas like what other people are thinking. This capacity, known as the Theory of Mind, enables us to comprehend irony, formulate ideas like morality, and forecast the behaviour of others.

The Quran has made references to man's special status as a sentient, logical being that sets him apart from other animals for over fifteen centuries. According to the Quran, written more than 1400 years ago, man was born with a great mind (cognitive tract), the ability to speak and reason, and free will.

> *Allah (SWT) says: "The Beneficent Hath made known the Qur'an, He hath created man, He hath taught him speech (and intelligence)" (Quran 55:1-4)*

According to the Quran, man has been given advantages above all other species, including intelligence, and the entire cosmos has been used for his benefit.

In a similar vein, a child's emotional well-being is critical to their growth and development and has a significant impact on maturity. Among the abilities that comprise emotional well-being is the capacity to understand and regulate emotions, form healthy and meaningful relationships, and cope with adversity. It's also imperative to understand the vital role of emotional well-being and how it impacts a child's cognitive, social, and general development.

Islamic Perspective on Mental and Emotional Strength

Early childhood cognitive development is about building the groundwork for all subsequent learning and problem-solving, not merely memorising facts. The Islamic definition of cognitive development goes beyond a person's ability to effectively manipulate and adapt to their surroundings; it also includes their understanding of their Creator (Allah SWT), their sense of their rights and obligations to Him, and the degree to which they are fulfilled in terms of worship. The following stages of cognitive development can be extracted from the Quranic verses and hadith:

Sinnul idrak al-Hissi

The five sense organs, which transmit information to the mind, are the primary means of sensory perception. At the beginning of this stage, the mind is empty, or "tabula rasa," to use Lockean terminology. The mind then employs its limited maturity and experience to comprehend and store the information. At this stage, the primary characteristics of behaviour are reflexive and instinctive inclinations, which are intrinsic and inborn (species behaviour). Gradually voluntary behaviours gradually replace these tendencies as ongoing contact with the environment occurs.

> *"It is He Who brought you forth from the wombs of your mothers when you knew nothing, and He gave you hearing, sight, and hearts that you might give thanks"* (Quran 16:78)

Attufulatul-Mubakkirah

Consider Verse 5 of Surah An-Nisa (Chapter 4): To those who lack comprehension (are weak-minded), do not take over your property. Famous and well-known exegetists like Ibn Abbas have interpreted the words "those weak of understanding" as young infants.

The Hadith, in which the Prophet (PBUH) commanded that children at the age of seven be enjoined to pray, serves as the foundation for defining the climbing age limit for this stage at that age. According to this Hadith, a child has finished one stage of his mental development and is entering a new one by the time he reaches the seventh year. In light of this, the seventh age thus becomes a boundary.

Sinnul-Murahaqah

At this stage, a child's cognitive development begins to take on a more structured form, laying the foundation for abstract thinking.

However, they are still within the realm of a child's mindset and have not yet reached full intellectual maturity. Because of this, they have not reached the Islamic concept of mukallaf—where a person becomes fully accountable for their actions.

Sinnul-Bulugh

A child's physical and cognitive development undergoes a sea change as they reach puberty. When a child reaches puberty, it is understood that they have attained a stage of mature cognitive development. For this reason, as soon as they reach puberty, all responsibilities become immediately compulsory. All of their actions and activities are now their responsibility. Therefore, it will now be noted by angels against him whenever they commit any wrongdoing.

Sinnu Bulugil Ashadd

Full development of the intellect (ages 33 to 40) The following passage that supports the demarcation of this stage is:

> *"Until, when he reaches the age of full strength and attains forty years, he says, 'My Lord, enable me to be grateful for Your favour which You have bestowed upon me and upon my parents, and to work righteousness that will please You, and make my descendants righteous. Indeed, I have repented to You, and indeed, I am of the Muslims.'"(Quran 46:15)*

Sinnul Tawaqquf

Cognitive decline is thought to begin around 40, and even if it does occur, it's very subtle and scarcely perceptible. For this reason, some academics have dubbed this stage Sinnul-Tawaqquf, which denotes a stage in which neither the decline nor any additional progressive development of mental functioning is discernible. It's more appropriately referred to as the age of constancy in mental growth. However, a person's mental functions continue to function normally during this stage. And beyond 80 years, mental deterioration becomes much more noticeable, especially as people age and reach 100 years of age or more.

Recognising Children's Emotional Health

In children's development, emotional well-being is a mental health condition in which kids can comprehend, communicate, and effectively control their emotions. Several important characteristics define emotional well-being:

- Self-esteem: A strong sense of confidence and worth in oneself.

- Empathy: The ability to comprehend and experience another person's emotions.

- Resilience: The capacity to bounce back from failures and adjust to new situations.

- Emotional regulation: The ability to manage and respond to emotions in a healthy manner.

Building a solid foundation for general well-being requires fostering optimal emotional development from birth through adolescence. During these crucial developmental stages, children learn vital emotional and social skills that affect how they behave and interact in the future. Children who receive early and continuous emotional development support are better able to create meaningful connections, cope with stress, and have a stable and healthy self-concept.

Hence, cognitive, social, and emotional development are all important aspects of raising strong kids. Islamic teachings strongly emphasise knowledge, morality, and responsibility while highlighting disciplined cognitive growth. A well-rounded approach gives kids the self-assurance, discernment, and life skills they need to succeed.

Chapter Three

Building a Strong Foundation of Faith

Instilling Islamic Beliefs and Values

Muslim children encounter particular difficulties navigating their faith, cultural backgrounds, and identity in today's quickly evolving world. Social pressures, cultural misinterpretations, and the ever-present influence of social media could cause these difficulties. On the other hand, giving kids a strong Muslim identity can foster a feeling of purpose, perseverance, and unshakeable devotion to their faith. Developing a thorough understanding of Islam at a young age is the first and most important stage in creating a solid Muslim identity.

> *Allah says in the Quran: "O you who have believed, protect yourselves and your families from a Fire whose fuel is people and stones." (Quran 66:6)*

As Muslim parents, we should aim to teach our children about the life of Prophet Muhammad (PBUH), the importance of the Quran, and the five pillars of Islam.

At home, we're the first to teach our children. First, Allah's (SWT) mercy, followed by our prayers, degree of adherence to Islam, and our example, will lead them to Islam and submission to Allah (SWT).

Daily routines like prayer (Salah) and fasting (Sawm) might help children develop discipline and a closer relationship with Allah (SWT). Children who engage in these activities can gain a solid foundation of faith that they can draw upon during trying times and comprehend the spiritual components of who they are.

Bring up the fundamentals with them. The Quran is our book (of guidance), Muhammad (PBUH) is our Prophet, Allah (SWT) is our Lord, and Islam is our way of life. By sharing and reminding them of this short sentence regularly, we can maintain their spiritual ties to Allah (SWT).

Just as the Prophet Muhammad (PBUH) is a model for us, we must be the shepherds of our families and set an example.

> *Abdullah Ibn Umar reported that the Prophet (PBUH) said: "Every one of you is a shepherd and is responsible for his flock. The leader of the people is a guardian and is responsible for his subjects. A man is the guardian of his family and he is responsible for them. A woman is the guardian of her husband's home and his children and she is responsible for them. The servant of a man is a guardian of the property of his master and he is responsible for it. No doubt, every one of you is a shepherd and is responsible for his flock." (Sahih Muslim)*

So, early Islamic education is crucial for a child to develop morally and to have a strong religious bond. From a young age, parents can inculcate qualities like integrity, empathy, and resilience by teaching basic Islamic principles in an interesting and age-appropriate way. Faith plays a vital role in everyone's life. It helps us comprehend the meaning and purpose of our existence and provides us with consolation, courage, and hope during difficult times. Faith shouldn't be reserved for adults. Early religious education is very important for children at an early age. Let's look at a few of the most important things that should be considered when teaching our children about faith and religion.

Teaching Tawhid (Monotheism) in Allah

Islam's monotheism serves as the cornerstone upon which all other doctrines and customs must be built. The root "wa-ha-da" from which we get the word "one," is the source of the verbal noun "monotheism" (Tawhid), which means "to make one."

According to this viewpoint, Islam's monotheism affirms that the Creator is one regarding His Lordship, His unassailable right to worship, and His divine titles and qualities. It also rejects any analogy between Him and His creation. All beliefs have their roots in Tawhid. One cannot become a Muslim without believing in Tawhid, just as a tree survives due to its roots rather than its branches.

Tawhid is the belief that Allah (SWT) Being is superior to having partners connected with Him in His Being and Attributes; in other words, it's the rejection of the idea that anyone is as God as Allah Almighty. A polytheist is someone who thinks that another can share Divine Attributes.

> *The Quran says: "They have certainly disbelieved who say, 'Allah is the third of three.' And there is no god except one God. And if they do not desist from what they are saying, there will surely be a painful punishment to those who disbelieve among them." (Quran 5:73)*

Children have a tendency to accept the Truth (Fitrah) from birth. When explaining an abstract idea to young children, it's very simple to overthink things. In actuality, however, half the work is already done. We're naturally drawn to the truth when born because Allah (SWT) created us in a clean state.

> *The Prophet (PBUH) said: "Every child is born with a true faith of Islam (i.e. to worship none but Allah Alone), and his parents convert him to Judaism or Christianity or Magianism, as an animal delivers a perfect baby animal. Do you find it mutilated?" (Sahih Bukhari)*

The only thing left to do as parents is to encourage our children's innate tendency to accept reality. This is accomplished by teaching children morality in conformity with the teachings of the Book of Allah (SWT) Quran and our Prophet (PBUH).

Start introducing your child to the beauty and wonder of Allah (SWT) in a way that's engaging and easy to understand from them. You can begin by teaching your child the fundamentals. Children often ask questions regarding the origin of existence because it's human nature to wonder where you're from and what created the world we all live in. You have a fantastic opportunity to explain to them why Allah (SWT) exists. You don't need to get into philosophical detail just yet; just summarise Allah's (SWT) primary attributes to them.

Given that children cannot perceive or imagine Allah (SWT) in any way, how do we bring Him to them? The best course of action is to assist them in observing Allah's creations. Demonstrate to them that the existence of creations can only indicate the existence of a Creator. Encourage them to take in their surroundings and start a basic conversation. Inform them that Allah (SWT) is the creator of everything, including these surrounding things. Another option is asking children questions like "Who created the sun and the sky?". Encourage them to reflect on Allah's (SWT) creations by asking them questions, "Do you think this car can come out of nowhere? Or has it been made by someone? The animals and trees also don't appear out of thin air. Allah (SWT) is the creator of all of them."

The three facets of Tawhid (the Oneness of Allah)—Tawhid Rububiyyah, Uluhiyyah, and Asma' wa Sifat—can then be introduced to them. Teaching children about these three categories is a straightforward way to help them learn about Allah (SWT).

Tawhid Rububiyyah (Oneness of Lordship) – This means believing that Allah (SWT) alone is the Creator, Sustainer, and Controller of everything in existence. He gives life and death, provides for all creatures, and has complete authority over the universe.

Tawhid Uluhiyyah (Oneness of Worship) – This means that only Allah (SWT) deserves to be worshipped, and all acts of worship, such as prayer, supplication, and sacrifice, should be directed to Him alone. Worshipping anything or anyone besides Allah (SWT) is considered shirk (associating partners with Him).

Tawhid Asma' wa Sifat (Oneness of Allah's Names and Attributes) – This means affirming all of Allah's (SWT) names and attributes as mentioned in the Quran and Sunnah without changing, denying, or comparing them to His creation. Allah (SWT) is unique, and His attributes, such as mercy, power, and knowledge, are perfect and incomparable.

You can teach a child of practically any age some of the most important attributes of Allah (SWT), like these. If your child is older and more curious, go further and explain that it's the responsibility of every Muslim to adhere to the principles that Allah (SWT) has established in the Quran and through the guidance of the prophets.

Increasing their understanding of Allah (SWT) might mean learning about His names; teaching your children about Allah's (SWT) names and attributes is wise if you wish for them to recognise His grandeur and power. This will inevitably foster a mentality in them that they should consistently trust and rely on Him. There are three stages to exploring Allah's (SWT) names. They are:

- To invoke Allah (SWT) with these names
- To comprehend their significance and how we might use them in our daily lives
- To commit the names to memory

Living and loving Islam naturally entails loving the Messenger who introduced us to this lovely faith. Teaching children about the life of the Prophet (PBUH) and instilling a love for Him (seerah) will help them develop a love for Allah (SWT).

Storytelling is another excellent method to introduce your child to the concept of Allah (SWT). Stories from the Quran and the teachings of the Prophet Muhammad (PBUH) abound throughout Islam, highlighting the qualities of Allah (SWT) and the significance of faith and good acts. Your child's imagination will be captured, and more abstract ideas will be easier for them to understand if you tell these stories in an easy-to-follow, captivating manner.

The story of the Prophet Ibrahim and how his everlasting faith in Allah (SWT) resulted in miraculous happenings in his life is an excellent example of a story you may share. Stories like these can help children learn about the strength and mercy of Allah (SWT) in a way that genuinely resonates with their comprehension level.

When you introduce Allah (SWT) to your kids, there are many chances for development, comprehension, and bonding. By beginning with the fundamentals, you can lead your kids on a journey of spiritual enlightenment and discovery. Don't forget to foster an atmosphere of love and inquiry where people may ask questions and share their expertise.

Encouraging love for the Prophet Muhammad (PBUH) and following his example

We all adore our Prophet (PBUH) because he is known as the blessing, giving us divine direction and greatly aiding us in discovering the truth.

> *"And we have not sent you, [O Muhammad], except as a mercy to the worlds."(Quran 21:107)*

Knowing that no other person has examined his life as thoroughly and meticulously as our Beloved Prophet (PBUH) is an incredible realisation! All aspects of his life have been documented. And in every way, He (PBUH) is the best example.

> *"Indeed, in the Messenger of Allah, you have an excellent example for whoever has hope in Allah and the Last Day and remembers Allah often." (Quran 33:21)*

Therefore, as Muslims, it should be natural for us to nurture the love of the Prophet (PBUH) in our children. Additionally, we ought to ensure that his love blossoms in our hearts daily. Our devotion to the Prophet (PBUH) ought to inspire us to live by the admirable rules he established. We cannot claim to love the honourable Prophet (PBUH) while acting in ways that are in direct opposition to his teachings.

Our children can be taught to adore the Prophet (PBUH) in a variety of ways, including:

Embodying the Prophetic character in our own interactions and acts is one of the best ways to teach our children to adore the Prophet (PBUH). When we live our lives with love, compassion, and moral behaviour, we provide a strong example for our children to follow.

Youngsters enjoy stories, so reading to them and conversing with them about the material fosters a love for the Prophet (PBUH), gives them time to spend with you, and strengthens your bond.

Furthermore, regularly reciting Darood Sharif (PBUH) and Salawat (blessings) as a family cultivates a spiritual atmosphere that nurtures love for the Prophet (PBUH). Our children's admiration and respect for the Beloved Messenger (PBUH) by encouraging their participation in events that celebrate the Prophet's (PBUH) love and praise.

Another way to nurture a love for the Prophet (PBUH) is to sit at a table with a large blank outline of Arabia, colours, and a guidebook outlining his life and travels. Begin the conversation by marking the location and date of the Prophet's (PBUH) birth on the paper. Encourage your children to colour a map representing the Prophet's (PBUH) life and label significant events as you discuss them. This map would include his residences, travel destinations, and other notable occurrences.

To worship Allah (SWT) and do Dhikr (Remembrance of Allah SWT), the Prophet (PBUH) would rise each day before dawn (Fajr). He would read the final verse of Surah Al-'Imran while gazing up at the sky, contemplating the cosmos and its Creator. This is a great method to become closer to Allah (SWT) when our focus is at its best, our brains are free of everyday concerns, and Allah (SWT) is very near to us. Encourage children to rise early enough to offer this unique habit on a Saturday or Sunday. Urge them to glorify Allah (SWT) by staying up as they can, just like the Prophet (PBUH).

Encourage children to participate in charitable and service projects inspired by the guidance of the Prophet (PBUH), which can also help them comprehend and assimilate the core of his teachings. Their love for the Prophet (PBUH) can be deepened by instructing them to embody the Prophetic qualities of mercy, charity, and empathy towards others. Fostering a love for the Prophet (PBUH) includes teaching them to appreciate recitation and dhikr, as well as other Prophetic etiquettes, such as how to enter a home, eat, and sleep.

Creating a Supportive Spiritual Environment

Are you aware that children who practise spirituality are more likely to have good mental health? Yes, it's true. Spirituality is directly connected to nature, a global presence, and a greater power. Anxiety and sadness may be overcome, much like physical well-being. Similarly, spiritual awareness cultivates the power of meditation, which inherently improves mental health and fosters optimism.

It's challenging to push your kids towards religion and force them to comprehend spirituality. However, if you create an atmosphere in your house that encourages spirituality, your child will naturally learn about it without coercion. The next concern is creating an environment in your home that will encourage spirituality.

A spiritual house is a haven where Islamic principles are maintained, and faith is fostered. The foundation of a child's spiritual and moral growth in Islam is the household, where they are initially exposed to their religion. Mothers are crucial in forming this environment as their children's primary teachers and role models. Creating a spiritual home is a journey, including devotion, love, and faith.

This path for Muslim mothers entails integrating the teachings of the Holy Prophet (PBUH) and the Quran into the very fabric of their family life. Fathers also play a significant role in nurturing a spiritual home, even though mothers frequently take the lead in this regard. Fathers reinforce mothers' morals and lessons by providing essential support and guidance.

A more coherent and consistent environment is produced for children when the mother and father collaborate to carry out instruction. Children are more likely to take their religious education seriously when observing both parents actively participating in it. The narrative of Hazrat Maryam (RA), the mother of Hazrat Isa (AS), a prime example of piety, endurance, and devotion, demonstrates how women are highly esteemed in the Quran. Muslim mothers are urged to emulate her by lovingly and devotedly fostering their children's spiritual growth.

Incorporating Regular Prayers (Salah) and Quran Recitation into Daily Life

In Islamic parenting, setting a good example is essential. Children are more likely to follow in their parent's footsteps when they see them doing that on a regular basis, for example, praying, reciting and acting politely. A parent's dedication to their spiritual development encourages their kids to follow in their footsteps.

Given the importance of prayer (salah), it's crucial to instil a love of it in children to secure the welfare of future generations of Muslims. Prayer or salah is a direct channel of connection between a person and Allah (SWT). Five times a day, Muslims offer salah, which promotes a daily rhythm of devotion and memory. This practice fosters discipline, attention, and a sense of community and strengthens one's spiritual foundation.

Prophet Muhammad (PBUH) stressed the value of forming moral values in children at an early age. Early exposure can develop a natural affinity for prayer in children, and as they age, it becomes an essential part of who they are. In addition to encouraging spiritual development, this gives children the skills to face life's obstacles head-on with courage and faith.

In Islam, Salah is a basic prayer act offered five times daily. Muslims use it as a direct line of connection with Allah (SWT) to pray for pardon, thank Him, and seek His guidance. As an indication of the Divine presence throughout the day, the prayers consist of an organised sequence of motions and recitations, such as standing, bowing, and prostrating. Every prayer is said at a certain time. These periods function as frequent opportunities to re-establish a spiritual centre and a connection with Allah (SWT):

- Fajr: Before dawn
- Dhuhr: After midday
- Asr: Mid-afternoon
- Maghrib: Just after sunset
- Isha: Night

Teaching children about Salah is a vital part of nurturing their Islamic faith and spiritual growth. By making the process engaging and meaningful, we can help them establish a profound connection with Allah (SWT) that will serve as their compass throughout their lives. Children can learn the significance of prayer and its advantages in this life and the next by incorporating enjoyable activities, regular routines, and concise explanations.

Children's devotion to and comprehension of Salah will grow as they mature, influencing their moral principles, self-control, and sense of direction. If we show our children love, patience, and direction, we may assist them in accepting Salah as a valued aspect of their everyday lives.

Furthermore, mothers can create a spiritual environment by introducing Islamic ideas into casual discussions. For example, talking about the importance of fasting during Ramadan or the benefits of generosity can help kids see how their faith is used in real-world situations.

Create a space anywhere in the house conducive to prayer to feel calmer and more spiritual. By structuring their homes according to Islamic principles, mothers can strengthen their own as well as their children's religion. A dedicated prayer space can feature soft carpets, high-quality flooring, and sound screens to reduce echoes. Post clear signs indicating the direction of Qibla and the times of prayer. These components contribute to creating a serene and spiritual environment.

Moreover, the Quran is a thorough manual for leading a moral life, not merely a religious document. It provides insight into many facets of human life, including morality, ethics, social behaviour, and individual accountability. Mothers must comprehend and apply these teachings in a way that fits with their family's daily schedule to genuinely foster a spiritual household. For example, the Quran instils principles that can be applied to daily encounters, such as honesty, patience, and compassion.

Mothers may foster an environment where children naturally exhibit these values by intentionally implementing these concepts. Incorporating lessons from the Quran into everyday life doesn't have to be difficult. Reflecting on a passage during family meals, talking about its significance, and coming up with ideas for using it throughout the day can be as easy as that.

Family time is a great way to reinforce the lessons found in the Quran. Families can improve their understanding of Islam and fortify their relationship by setting aside particular times for Quranic study and contemplation. Including stories from the Quran in nighttime rituals is one strategy. For instance, the narratives of the Prophets are full of moral teachings and can be an effective means of imparting virtues like endurance, bravery, and faith in Allah (SWT). Mothers can spark their children's imaginations and provide valuable lessons by telling these stories engrossingly.

Regular study sessions are another good approach to include lessons from the Quran in family time. Simply reading a few passages aloud and then discussing their meaning and relevance to current affairs or individual experiences can serve as the basis for these sessions. Including kids in these conversations fosters critical thinking skills and enables them to relate the Quran's lessons to their personal experiences.

Choose a room in your house that is conducive to learning and free from interruptions. To create a calm and motivating ambience, this space can be embellished with Islamic art, calligraphy, or pictures of the Kaaba. Having a specific area for studying the Quran and offering prayers teaches kids the value of these times and inspires them to approach the text respectfully. This area doesn't need to be ornate; even a tiny, peaceful nook can be used as a haven for studying and contemplating spirituality.

Thus, you must begin teaching your child everything you want them to learn at home. If you want your children to learn about and believe in the Creator, create a spiritual atmosphere at home. Therefore, be sure to adhere to the methods mentioned above to create an atmosphere that will enable you to teach your child about the ultimate power and strengthen your faith in Him.

Chapter Four

Encouraging Emotional Intelligence and Resilience

Understanding Emotional Intelligence

Imagine the following situation: A boy named Abdul Salam is having trouble with his arithmetic assignment. Rather than shouting and giving up, he confides in his mother about his frustration and for assistance. Or this one: Abdul Salam's friend cancels their plans to hang out after receiving some distressing news. Abdul Salam can see why his friend makes other plans and doesn't feel like interacting with others. These answers may not seem significant. However, they are indicators of a significant collection of abilities that comprise "emotional intelligence" (EI).

One aspect of social intelligence is emotional intelligence (EI), also known as emotional quotient (EQ), which includes the capacity to track one's and other people's emotions, distinguish between various emotions, and use emotional data to shape decisions and actions. An individual can recognise, assess, regulate, comprehend, communicate, and handle emotions in constructive ways for themselves, others, and their relationships. Academic intelligence is measured by IQ, and emotional intelligence is measured by EQ.

Children of various ages can learn and develop this set of abilities. Youngsters can gain emotional intelligence skills but require adult guidance and training, particularly from parents. Emotions affect our mental and physical health as well as all other areas of our lives. Gaining emotional intelligence makes it possible to successfully control emotions and prevent them from getting out of control, like when one gets angry.

Awareness, comprehension, and the capacity to express and control one's emotions are all components of emotional intelligence. It has been viewed as the ability to perform under duress, the confidence in effective relationships, the bravery to make choices, and the foresight to shape the future.

Consider the difficulties Abdul Salam may encounter on a daily basis. He can struggle with tasks that are simple for his peers. Despite his best efforts, he still receives low grades. He might be scared to ask for assistance because he feels ashamed of his learning disabilities.

Emotional intelligence has a crucial influence in determining our approach to problems. When Abdul Salam has learning and thought disparities, emotional intelligence (EI) can act as a GPS to guide him through challenges and toward achievement. It enables him to assess circumstances, put them in perspective, and devise solutions.

Emotional intelligence is not a problem for many children with learning and cognitive difficulties. In reality, some people have exceptionally high EI. However, difficulties with EI might occasionally be a precursor to a child's learning or cognitive differences.

Due to their inability to pay close enough attention, children with ADHD may fail to notice social signs. Children with auditory processing issues may misunderstand what other people say. Additionally, children with nonverbal learning difficulties may not be able to understand social cues at all. Conversely, it's not unusual for dyslexics to exhibit extremely high EI. According to some studies, this might be because of their brain's innate capacity for "big picture" thinking.

Islam promotes emotional intelligence. Many of the teachings of the Prophet Muhammad (PBUH) emphasise empathy, compassion, introspection, and effective communication. In accordance with Islamic teachings, parents can raise emotionally intelligent children by embracing these ideals.

The application and growth of emotional intelligence can benefit greatly from Islamic ideas. For instance, the Quran mention empathy and self-control as:

> *"And march forth in the way (which leads to) forgiveness from your Lord, and for Paradise as wide as the heavens and the earth, prepared for Al-Muttaqun (the pious)."* (Quran 3:133). *"Those who spend (freely), whether in prosperity or in adversity, who repress anger, and who pardon men; verily, Allah loves Al-Muhsinun (the good-doers)."(Quran 3:134)*

Several resources in the Sunnah promote emotional intelligence. One instance of empathy is seen in the following quote from the Prophet Muhammad (PBUH):

> *"None of you truly believes until he wishes for his brother (Muslims call each other brother/sister) what he wishes for himself."* And in self-control and self-management, the prophet said: *"Powerful is not he who knocks the other down, indeed powerful is he who controls himself in a fit of anger." (Sahih Bukhari)*

Emotional intelligence is comprised of five components:

Self-awareness: The ability to recognise one's own emotions and how they impact other people. An essential component of emotional control is self-awareness. It serves as the foundation for the other components of emotional intelligence.

Self-regulation: The ability to control one's own emotions and how they are expressed. This is crucial for forecasting children's success. Children with good self-control will be more successful and healthy, have better grades, and have fewer bad records.

Motivation: Despite any unfavourable emotions, a person can achieve his aims. They understand what matters in life.

Empathy: The capacity to comprehend the emotions of others. People with emotional intelligence are sympathetic. They are adept at considering problems from several angles and putting themselves in other people's shoes.

Social Skills: The ability to establish and maintain relationships. These varied abilities are employed to elicit favourable reactions from other people. Demonstrating positive emotions to others is a component of social skills.

These five essential components are typically present in people with high EI. Together, these five components enable Abdul Salam to attain the greatest result. When he's having trouble with the math assignment, that could look like this:

- He becomes aware of his frustration.
- He thinks about the consequences of shouting or dropping his book on the ground right away.
- He is motivated to try again despite his frustration because he sees the long-term benefits.
- He asks his mother for assistance.

- He says he would like to attempt it again and that he should take it slow.

- He realises that his mother tries a bit too hard because she genuinely cares about him and wants to see him succeed.

- He waits until after class the following day to inform his teacher that he cannot grasp it.

> *"And do not be like those who forgot Allah, so He made them forget themselves. Those are the defiantly disobedient" (Quran 59:19)*

This verse highlights the importance of self-awareness, as forgetting oneself leads to misguidance. Recognising one's emotions, like Abdul Salam realising his frustration, is a key part of self-awareness.

Thus, emotional intelligence (EI) was a navigator to help Abdul Salam overcome obstacles and reach his goals when facing difficulties. It helped him evaluate situations, put them in perspective, and develop solutions. Emotional intelligence allows one to consider the emotional state of others to motivate, plan, and accomplish one's goals. That's why it's a set of abilities kids must acquire at any age.

Children grow more self-aware as they learn to recognise their feelings. They can better comprehend how they respond to various circumstances because of their increased self-awareness. Since it establishes the groundwork for social interactions and individual well-being, emotional intelligence development is crucial for children.

Additionally, emotional intelligence is important for leadership and teamwork, two lifelong talents. Youngsters with high EQ are frequently more resilient and adaptive, making it easier to handle difficulties and transitions.

Teaching Children to Recognise and Express their Emotions

An essential component of a child's overall development is their ability to comprehend and control their emotions. Emotions greatly influence a child's behaviour, social interactions, and general well-being. Early emotional education helps prepare children to handle obstacles, build positive connections, and communicate clearly.

Emotions are like stones in an imaginary rucksack, especially heavy ones like sadness, rage, and concern. They will weigh us down and burden our children if we do not release them. Conversely, we can create a safe space for our kids to genuinely feel and let go of their emotions if we embrace them, stay close, and offer them love, even when they cry and act out. The rucksack feels significantly lighter after emotions are expressed, and our children are noticeably different—they appear lighter, more affectionate, more cooperative, and generally happier.

Never forget that children are not born with the ability to recognise and communicate their emotions. It's something they have to practise and develop over time, just like reading or riding a bike. Children who learn to recognise and positively express their emotions are better equipped to deal with them in the future.

Since the family is the most important social unit in which children are reared, the family environment has a significant impact on how a child develops their personality. It's one of the most significant social settings where children acquire a variety of beliefs, behaviours, and life-adapting skills. A healthy personality will be fostered in a family setting full of trust and loyalty, as opposed to one filled with arguments and bickering.

Parents have a big impact on how their children's personalities. They can be the best teachers for their own children and naturally desire the best for them. To help their children succeed in life, they should be prepared to educate them on emotional intelligence. Parenting can be challenging, and children often require extensive care and support. Parents need not be "super-parents," concealing their emotions from their kids. It's essential for children to learn from their parents how to manage their emotions and behave appropriately when they are away from home.

The good news is that it's possible to teach emotion recognition at an earlier age than you may imagine. Even before they can speak, children can begin learning these skills! We can teach children emotional terms from birth, like colours, ABCs, and numbers.

Your child will become a better leader, citizen, and parent if you help them develop emotional intelligence now. The following few pointers will assist parents in becoming their children's "emotion coach" and teaching them about emotions:

Name the Emotion

One of the fundamental skills children learn early in life is identifying and differentiating between various emotions. Most children can differentiate between major emotions, including anger, fear, sadness, and happiness, as early as six months. They acquire the ability to interpret body language, tone of voice, and faces to distinguish between various emotional states in those around them.

We must teach children the words to connect with these feelings when their language skills develop. A child who receives assistance developing their emotional language will better grasp how to communicate their feelings through words. As they grow older, they discover more distinct feelings, such as delight, contempt, and frustration. They can also discover that most feelings have more nuanced forms, such as the distinction between pride, happiness, joy, satisfaction, and ecstasy.

Encouraging kids to express their feelings through dua (supplication) and patience (sabr) helps them understand that all emotions are part of Allah's (SWT) divine wisdom. Additionally, using stories from the

Quran and the Prophet's (PBUH) life can help them recognise and manage emotions with empathy, gratitude, and self-control.

Assisting Children in Identifying their Emotions

We must recognise our emotions in real time and comprehend how they impact our thoughts and actions before we can express and control them, much like children do. Many people struggle to identify their feelings when they're happening, which might lead them to do something they later regret. Using these exercises, you may educate kids to identify their feelings in real-time, enabling them to apply improved coping mechanisms, communication, and expression as needed.

It can be challenging to learn to recognise our feelings in the present moment. After a difficult situation, discuss what transpired once your child is calm. Ask them to describe their physical sensations and emotions. Personal examples can also be used to normalise this conversation. Encourage your children to write or illustrate in a daily emotion journal about the feelings they are experiencing at the time and the day's events. Urge them to explain how they understood their feelings and how their body felt at that exact moment.

Encourage your children to illustrate objects or circumstances that bring them joy, sorrow, rage, anxiety, etc. Ask about their drawings and discuss how they were aware of the emotion. Assist them with recalling specific instances in which they typically feel a certain feeling, such as seeing a close friend (happy/excited), having a sibling take a toy away from them (angry/mad) or being dropped off at school (nervous/worried). They will be able to identify these feelings earlier in life.

Remember that you want to teach your child to recognise emotions early on so they can make more deliberate decisions rather than allowing their feelings to rule them. Adults must initially make the majority of the effort, but as time goes on, you'll see that kids can express their emotions sooner and take action. Begin teaching children how to communicate their feelings as soon as they are able to recognise them in the moment.

Assisting Children with Proper Emotional Expression

It's critical that kids learn how to express their emotions once they have mastered emotion terminology and begin to observe how they feel in the moment. This can be challenging because kids may inadvertently learn that we should suppress some feelings, such as grief, loneliness, or rage. "Stop crying," "You need to calm down," or "It could be a lot worse" are some examples of what parents may say.

Rather, kids should be taught that everyone feels a variety of emotions as a normal part of life and that expressing any feelings is okay. Making time to discuss emotions and normalising all sentiments is the best method to educate children on how to express them.

As parents, it's important to make it a habit to talk to your children. Make time each day to talk, even if it's only for a little while. They will understand that you are there to help them, that you care, and are listening. By having conversations with our children, we can learn more about how they feel and perceive their surroundings.

As parents, express your emotions and let them know it's acceptable for them to follow suit. Additionally, remember that kids are still developing their self-control, so they might still act out occasionally. Reacting with more bad emotions doesn't help when kids misbehave to express rage, grief, or any other tough emotion. Show empathy and make an effort to mentor them towards more effective self-expression.

Supporting Children in Handling Strong Emotions

Everyone has intense feelings from time to time. For this reason, it's important that we educate children on how to regulate their emotions. We want them to understand that although these feelings are natural and acceptable, we nevertheless need to be in charge of our decisions and actions. Naming emotions, being aware of them at all times, and expressing them in an acceptable way are all components of emotion control.

One of the simplest and most effective coping mechanisms that children can learn is how to practise deep belly breathing. Breathing gives us a moment to pause and slows down the neurological system. Breathing exercises should be performed regularly, not only when a child is agitated but also right before bed. Furthermore, meditation and mindfulness exercises can also assist in children's development of this ability.

A vital component of good emotions is social and familial interactions. Your child should be encouraged to think of someone they can confide in and feel at ease with. Have them write a list, perhaps! They can contact someone on their list if they're feeling unhappy. Sometimes, we just need to distract ourselves from the problem.

Ask your child to select their favourite diversionary activity, such as sketching, slime play, or watching a funny video. It's helpful to return to a situation and discuss it with them to help them comprehend and address problems after they have briefly paused and calmed down.

Although it takes time, managing intense emotions is a crucial growth process! Have patience as your child learns to stop and catch themselves when agitated. Keep in mind that we practise this skill throughout our lives.

Developing Empathy and Compassion through Islamic Teachings

Islam places a high value on children's moral and spiritual growth; instilling principles in children that will guide them throughout their lives, forming their character, bolstering their faith, and assisting them in forming healthy relationships is our duty as parents.

Raising children to be responsible, caring Muslims requires instilling Islamic ideals in them from an early age. As Muslims, one of the soft skills that our faith emphasises is empathy.

> *"None of you will have faith till he wishes for his (Muslim) brother what he likes for himself." (Sahih Bukhari)*

Islamic education fosters compassion, which in turn fosters empathy. Numerous verses of the Quran, the Holy Book of Islam, exhort individuals to have compassion for others.

> *"And be merciful to those on earth, and God will also be merciful to you." (Quran 2:222)*

Furthermore, Islamic education emphasises the importance of polite and courteous interactions with others. Youngsters learn to engage in respectful discussions about the cultures, beliefs, and lives of those around them. They are encouraged to treat one another with love, patience, and honesty. This approach enables individuals to understand diverse viewpoints, fostering the development of empathetic thinking.

Islamic traditions hold that parents are crucial in helping their children develop empathy. Parents can foster empathy in their kids by teaching their kids how to engage with others, modelling appropriate behaviour, and teaching them how to treat others with respect.

Here are some strategies to help your kids develop empathy:

Set a positive example: Since parents are viewed as their heroes, children learn best by watching them. Be kind to everyone in your home and in your everyday encounters, including your family, friends, neighbours, coworkers, store employees, and domestic help. Words are not as powerful as your deeds.

Promote deeds of kindness: Encourage your kids to serve others, share what they enjoy, and treat their classmates, siblings, and teachers with kindness. When kids demonstrate compassion, even in tiny ways, praise them. Insha'Allah, this encouragement will help kids develop a caring attitude and inspire them to be more kind and empathetic.

Read and discuss the Prophet's (PBUH) and his companions' stories: Throughout his life, the Prophet (PBUH) showed great compassion and mercy. Tell your kids about his compassion, including how he helped the weak, took care of animals, and forgave those who had harmed him. These tales are excellent resources for teaching empathy.

Teaching children Islamic principles like kindness and empathy is crucial to moulding their character and faith. By setting an example, telling tales of the prophets, and giving them chances to put these principles into practice, we may raise a generation that exemplifies these traits in their daily interactions. Ultimately, these principles will support our kids' development into resilient, responsible, and caring adults who uphold Islamic principles.

Fostering Resilience and Coping Skills

Giving kids the skills they need to overcome obstacles is crucial in today's complicated world. Developing children's resilience enhances their general well-being and helps them deal with challenges. Resilience is overcoming hardship, maintaining composure, and developing resilience in the face of difficulty.

Drawing from the Quran, the sayings of the Prophet Muhammad (PBUH), and current scientific findings, Islam offers us priceless advice on how to help children develop resilience.

Our duty as parents and educators is to equip our children with the skills necessary to navigate challenging situations in life. Children will inevitably have to face these harsh realities at some point in their lives, regardless of how much we attempt to shield them from the negativity and heartbreaks of the outside world. Fostering emotional and spiritual resilience entails imparting Allah's (SWT) wisdom and decree while supporting them in overcoming the calamities affecting people globally. Let's explore how we can address this:

Strategies for Helping Children Deal with Challenges and Setbacks

Obstacles and disappointments are inevitable in life, even for our young children. One of the best gifts we can give our kids as parents is the capacity to overcome hardship with fortitude. We would do almost anything to prevent our children from suffering since no parent enjoys witnessing them suffer. However, everyone must encounter disappointment, frustration, and blunders to develop effective coping mechanisms.

We frequently want to rapidly help our children deal with these uncomfortable feelings, divert their attention, or provide them with a comforting phase. Our mature, logical brain wants to solve the problem and assure them it's not a big concern. We're depriving our children of the opportunity to build resilience and, eventually, the confidence that they can conquer or survive setbacks when we don't let them go through the process.

When we must see our child suffer, how can we as parents not feel totally defeated? Although it's difficult, if we support our children through it, they will be far more prepared for adulthood than we were.

Resilience is the strong inner fortitude that enables children to adapt to stressful situations and confront challenging circumstances directly. By nurturing resilience in our children from a young age, we can provide them with invaluable coping mechanisms that will benefit them throughout their lives. The following strategies are beneficial:

Strengthen your Faith

As parents, we must acknowledge and teach our children that life will be difficult at times and that we must always turn to Allah (SWT) because sometimes we cannot accomplish a few things on our own without His guidance. Children learn that difficulties are a natural part of life but that there is always hope and relief after adversity when they are taught the strength of faith and dependence on Allah (SWT). Promoting consistent prayer, learning, and worship strengthens their faith and fortitude. Allah (SWT) reassures us:

> *"Verily, with every difficulty there is relief." (Quran 94:5)*

Practise Patience

Teaching kids the importance of patience gives them the strength to persevere through challenges and aim for greater results. One of the best methods to teach patience is to demonstrate it in everyday actions. Exhibit your ability to wait your turn, manage frustration, and react composedly to challenging situations. The goal of teaching children patience is to help them become resilient, compassionate, and well-rounded people, not just better kids.

Patient children learn the importance of postponing gratification, a maturity-enhancing skill. Impulsivity and acting out behaviours can be countered with patience, which can aid in the development of problem-solving and thinking skills.

> *"Indeed, Allah is with the patient" (Quran 2:153)*

This verse emphasises the relationship between spiritual strength and patience, highlighting the idea that patience is a divine trait that can help us become closer to Allah rather than just a human virtue.

Adopt Positive Thinking

For better or worse, our thoughts strongly influence how we feel and how we're feeling, which in turn influences how we act. Islam encourages us to focus our introspection (Tafakkur), or deep thinking, on Allah's (SWT) benefits and wonders, his names and qualities, our hope for the Hereafter, and our optimism. In addition to reducing the anger, sadness, and anxiety that worldly ideas cause, we can improve the efficacy of our prayers and worship by positively managing our mental processes.

Satan (the devil) will occasionally instil negative ideas in our thinking. Until we decide to take action, these recommendations have no influence over us. A terrible fate awaits us if we follow a bad or evil line of thought. Therefore, to counteract the negative impacts of a negative thought pattern, we must quickly replace it with a good inside remark.

Negative thinking results in anger, jealousy, hatred, anxiety, despair, and other pessimistic emotional states. These ideas are about the outside world, our money, our social standing, people we dislike or have mistreated, and so forth. The devotion to the illusions of materialism and worldly life, which veil the heart and hinder its cleansing, is the root source of these ideas.

Positive thinking results in good feelings, acts of kindness, peace of mind, thankfulness, calm, satisfaction, and other optimistic emotional states. These are sincere ideas regarding Allah (SWT), the prophets, the Hereafter, our bounties, our deeds, and so forth. In the heart, they generate insight and wisdom.

We must learn to focus our mental processes on constructive ideas and block out negative ones before they lead us into a downward spiral. Many of the Prophet's companions regarded the ability to positively guide one's thoughts as the enlightenment of genuine religion.

Given the numerous advantages of positivity, we're responsible as parents to instil in our children the Sunnah of the Prophet Muhammad

(PBUH), which advocates for optimistic thinking and the constant pursuit of the positive rather than the negative.

> *"Look at those who are lowers than you and do not look at those who are higher than you, lest you belittle the favors Allah conferred upon you" (Sahih Muslim)*

This reminder encourages us to instil the value of being thankful for what they have and finding the good in every circumstance.

Encourage Problem-Solving Skills

Islamic teachings strongly emphasise learning new things and coming up with workable answers. Children who are given the chance to think critically, make choices, and solve problems grow into more resilient problem solvers. Problem-solving abilities strengthen resilience and promote general mental health.

> *In the Quran, Allah (SWT) says: "And we have certainly created man to be in hardship" (Quran 90:4)*

Encourage to Learn from Failure

Children should be encouraged to view failures as opportunities for development and education rather than setbacks. Failure builds resilience when kids learn to recognise lessons, modify their approach, and persevere in the face of difficulty. We can successfully enable our children to develop resilience with the profound wisdom of Islamic teachings.

It's crucial to stress that resilience is about confronting obstacles head-on, believing that every struggle presents an opportunity for progress, and having faith in Allah (SWT). This hadith teaches the importance of learning from past experiences and being cautious:

"A believer is not bitten from the same hole twice" (Sahih Muslim)

Unity in Strength

Teach them more than ever the value of community in Islam, even when they may be having difficulties and feeling alone when seeing circumstances over which they believe they have control. Urge them to ask for assistance and support from others when necessary. Remind them of the togetherness and strength of belonging to one Ummah and the Muslim community. When children attend congregations or age-appropriate events at nearby mosques, they can experience this.

You may presume your children understand how much you value and love them. However, encouraging words are important, and kids need to feel safe and secure, particularly while exposed to life's difficulties. Remind your children they are loved and safe. Use explanations that are suitable for their comprehension level and age. Even more so, as Muslims, you can assist them in realising that despite the difficulties, people are striving to improve the world and trusting Allah (SWT) for better outcomes.

Moreover, give your child age-appropriate responsibility and have faith in them to make some decisions for themselves. They gain independence and improve their problem-solving abilities as a result. Keep the lines of communication open with your child so they can share their feelings and thoughts. Instead of telling them what to do, actively listen to them and offer advice when necessary.

It's a huge effort for parents to get the balance right in light of what we see. There is no one-size-fits-all solution, so don't punish yourself if you feel like you're not doing it right or meeting your standards. When attempting to traverse unfamiliar territory, exercise the same patience with yourself as you do with your kids.

Chapter Five

Effective Communication and Listening

Building Open Lines of Communication

Muslims believe that Allah (SWT) bestows human communication skills as a gift, as stated in the Quran:

> "He who created mankind. He also taught humans to communicate" (Quran 55:3-4)

Thus, it's human nature to communicate. Put another way, communication is essential to human existence and is a necessity in and of itself, meaning that it will persist for as long as people are alive.

Humans undoubtedly communicate 70% of the time they spend on a daily basis. Without communication, there would be no purpose to human existence. As a result, the human need for communication implies another human need: the need for closeness to other humans, which can only be attained through conversation. Naturally, if there is effective communication, this closeness will manifest. With effective communication, each relationship can blossom.

Family is one of the core areas of human existence where communication is necessary. A family is where parents, kids, and other family members interact. Building effective communication between parents and children will result in positive interactions between them. Establishing this kind of communication is not as simple but requires careful management.

Children's behaviour, development of their skills and interests, and attitudes and behaviour are all impacted by the communication between parents and children. As a result, parents must focus on their own and their children's communication. This is because effective, seamless, and transparent communication between parents and children will positively affect the children's attitudes, behaviour, and aspects of their abilities and interests, and vice versa.

Building a solid foundation that can support kids in overcoming obstacles in life requires positive parent-child connections. Effective communication is one of the most important elements in creating a solid parent-child bond. In addition to helping kids feel heard, acknowledged, and understood enables parents to comprehend their needs, feelings, and viewpoints. Effective communication between parents and children can improve their connection by fostering mutual respect, trust, and understanding. Families may establish a secure and caring atmosphere where kids feel free to express themselves and share their ideas and emotions when they speak honestly and openly.

Children may gain confidence and a sense of self-worth as a result. Parents who communicate well are also better able to respond to their children's demands. When they actively and attentively listen to their children, parents are better able to comprehend and meet their children's needs. A stronger sense of security and trust between parent and child may result from this.

Communication occurs in every interaction you have with your child. Not only do your words matter, but your tone of voice, gaze, hugs and kisses all send messages to your child. Your communication style with your child influences their emotional growth and future relationship-building in addition to teaching them how to interact with others.

As life is so hectic, many of us frequently feel as though we're juggling too many responsibilities. Our society demands that we feel as though we must "have it all" and pushes us to "multi-task" to varying degrees. What impact does this have on the way we raise our families? To help your kids feel valued and included in your relationship, keep the channels of communication open. Although there are many distractions in the world, we must prioritise and make our families and kids the greatest ones. Here are some small changes we can make to improve the quality of our interactions with our kids by facilitating communication.

Encouraging Children to Express their Thoughts and Feelings Openly

Encouraging children to identify, comprehend, and express their emotions is a crucial component of helping them communicate properly. Over time, this may benefit their behaviour, performance, drive to learn, and mental health.

Seeing things from your child's point of view is one of the first steps to enhancing communication. Young children, in particular, have a totally different perspective on the world than adults. They have strong emotions but are still learning to communicate verbally. When they act out or appear to ignore you, it's frequently a scream for explanation rather than resistance.

Islam places a high importance on love and patience, which you can show by understanding your emotions and recognising your difficulties. Feelings that are suppressed can lead to tension and stress in the body, and eventually, they will surface. This is why it's so crucial to teach children and teenagers how to express themselves successfully.

Set a good example and promote conversation. When you and your child or young person are engaged in other activities, such as going for a stroll, taking a car ride, painting or sketching together, or baking or cooking, good talks frequently occur. Young people and children frequently open up when engaged in other activities. Spend as much time as possible talking to each other. It might be challenging to encourage your child to open up at times, so set an example by opening up about your own day.

Using language that encourages your child to express their feelings and thoughts is an easy method to deal with their behaviour. Instead of using confrontational language like "What's the matter with you?" try asking them, "Can you help me understand more about how you feel?" These few sentences below will help your child better communicate their feelings and improve understanding.

"It's acceptable to feel like this. I'm available for a conversation whenever you'd like." Your child may occasionally require some time to open up because it can be challenging to experience bad feelings. Be sure to acknowledge their emotions in such a circumstance. Young people who feel safe and secure are more inclined to show their feelings without worrying about misinterpretation or scrutiny.

"No matter what, I'm always here for you." One of the greatest presents you can give your child is this phrase. Knowing that you're always there for them gives them a sense of security and strength and bravery to express their emotions.

"I notice that you're struggling with _____. What can we do to improve it?" When your child experiences minor discomfort, it's in our nature as parents to step in and save the day. It's crucial to promote critical thinking and problem-solving skills despite the temptation to immediately resolve the issue and when it's safe to do so.

Asking your child how we may fix their difficulties allows them to think about and create methods to tackle the root of their irritation. Acknowledging their difficulties encourages them to think about what has happened and how they are feeling. As a result, children will feel more equipped to tackle problems on their own or seek assistance when necessary.

Youngsters may not always express their emotions immediately, particularly when dealing with a difficult situation. It's crucial to address your child's recent behavioural change with empathy, comfort that you're there for them, and appreciation when they do express their emotions to you.

Active Listening Techniques to Understand and Support Children's Needs

Children can feel understood and heard when parents actively listen to them. Demonstrate your genuine interest in what your child is saying and your engagement with them by utilising gestures like affirming nods and encouraging smiles. Your child may feel more secure and attached to you if you can look them in the eye when they are speaking.

The best example of active listening is when a parent puts aside distractions and gives their child their whole attention when they're speaking. To demonstrate that you are paying attention, put phones and other electronics away and make eye contact. Young people are more inclined to open up and express their ideas and emotions when they see that their parents are paying attention.

Raising questions like "what?" "why?" and "how?" demonstrate that you're paying close attention to what they have to say. Educating your child on how to tell a tale and what details to add also helps them to become a better communicator. Parents may provide a secure and encouraging environment for their children to speak for themselves and feel heard by being present, focused, and sympathetic. Parents and children can develop a stronger connection and trust by actively listening to each other's needs and viewpoints.

Pay attention to these active listening three P's and R's:

Active listening's three Ps are:

- Listening in the present.
- Hearing from a perspective.
- Listening personas.

Active listening's three Rs are:

- **Respect** is the most basic etiquette and is where active listening starts.
- **Remind** yourself to take notes during your chat before it goes in one ear and out the other.
- **Review**: Always end a discussion or presentation with a summary, a course of action, the next steps, and any further actions that may be necessary.

Behaving like a mirror is another excellent approach to demonstrate to your child that you're interested in and attentive to what they have to say. Using alternative words, repeat back to you what they have said.

For instance, you could ask, "You're not playing with Bilal anymore?" in response to your child saying, "I'm not playing with Bilal anymore." This allows your child to express their feelings without fear of criticism. How much they have to say may surprise you!

Active listening demonstrates to your child your importance and appreciation for their ideas and emotions. The teachings of Prophet Muhammad (PBUH), who was renowned for giving his full attention to everybody who spoke to him, align with this strategy.

Using Positive Reinforcement

We sometimes reward children for good actions. This is known as positive reinforcement, which could be an instant reward or a star on a chart. One of the most crucial things to remember when using positive reinforcement is to acknowledge and commend the behaviour, not the child. Praising a child's actions or conversations rather than their personality fosters development increases their sense of self-efficacy, and helps them communicate effectively. This is because, in contrast to more innate personality qualities, they can learn new skills.

How to Recognise and Reward Positive Behaviours and Achievements?

Positive reinforcement can be provided in various methods tailored to your child's personality and how they express gratitude or affection. The goal is to increase the frequency of desired conduct by using positive reinforcement. Common examples include:

- Give them praise: Acknowledge and appreciate their efforts.
- Hugs and smiles
- Give thoughtful gifts: Reward them with their favourite things.
- Spend quality time: Engage in activities that are meaningful to them.

Children of all ages respond favourably to positive reinforcement since they want to please you and make wise decisions. When we praise them, children are encouraged to repeat these wise decisions. In operant conditioning, adding a reinforcing stimulus after a specific behaviour is known as positive reinforcement. For example, if a child communicates honesty with their parents instead of lying or hiding things, they may receive a reward such as a new toy or a special day out.

This reinforcement increases the likelihood that they will continue the behaviour in the future.

Positive reinforcement is favoured above punitive methods in Islamic parenting. Parents should encourage and reward excellent behaviour in addition to punishing misbehaviour. This strategy is consistent with the Islamic idea of promoting virtue.

> *The Prophet Muhammad (PBUH) said, "Whoever does not show mercy will not be shown mercy" (Sahih Bukhari)*

This hadith emphasises how crucial empathy and positive reinforcement are to good parenting. Children are more likely to repeat positive behaviours when they receive praise and rewards. The most important thing is to recognise and value your child's efforts and accomplishments, regardless of how minor they may appear.

Chapter Six

Discipline with Compassion and Fairness

Islamic Principles of Discipline

The term discipline comes from the Latin "to teach." Teaching your child self-control and responsible behaviour is the goal of discipline. Your kid will learn about results and accepting accountability for their own conduct if they receive consistent and appropriate discipline.

The ultimate goal is to help them learn how to control their emotions and behaviour. We refer to this as self-monitoring. In its finest form, discipline uses fair and constructive methods to discourage incorrect behaviour and promote acceptable behaviour.

Over time, a child's intellectual capacity grows. It's critical to align your child's disciplinary and comprehension levels. An infant, for example, is too young to understand the difference between right and wrong. However, as they start to mature, they'll develop an inbuilt need for protection, which is satisfied by the boundaries established by proper discipline, which offer safety and security.

Boundaries give children a sense of security and safety, which is essential for their emotional and cognitive development. When they feel comfortable, children can focus their energies on interacting with and investigating their surroundings. If such boundaries aren't established, children focus on negative testing behaviours. At this stage, the child is essentially pleading with you to stop them when testing gets out of control. This is when discipline comes into play.

Setting limits, instilling morals, and directing behaviour are all necessary components of discipline so children can grow up to be responsible adults. Since developing children are like a mould of clay, they'll take on the shape of whatever you shape them into; it's crucial to instil consistency in them while they're growing up.

Every child has the right to be disciplined by parents who are sensible. A parent guides their child through discipline and control. Humans are naturally inclined towards evil.

> *"Surely the soul is wont to command (towards) evil except, such as my Lord has mercy on" (Quran 12:53)*

Humans are prone to misconduct when they lack discipline. A child is particularly susceptible to these impulses because he lacks the maturity and insight of an adult.

Parents are the primary role models for children's character and personality development since children always tend to learn by watching others, especially their parents. The same may be said for their capacity to absorb parental correction. When parents prioritise maintaining a healthy, disciplined routine in their lives, they set an example for their kids—one that they may follow into adulthood and continue throughout their lives.

Therefore, discipline is a key component of the entire parenting process that moulds children's behaviour and character. It teaches kids how to handle life's ups and downs and prepares them for obstacles. Let's look at a few important aspects of teaching children discipline.

Overall Benefits of Discipline

Above all, discipline encourages kids to obey rules and show respect for authority. Without discipline, children are more likely to be disobedient and rebellious as adults, which can cause major issues. Parents and teachers can teach children the value of obeying rules and showing respect for authority by setting clear guidelines and penalties. Better behaviour in social settings, at home, and at school may result.

Children who get discipline may also develop a feeling of accountability. Children learn to accept responsibility for their mistakes while making amends when held accountable for their behaviour. As they learn to think about how their actions affect other people, this can aid them in developing empathy and a sense of justice. Children can feel a sense of control over their lives and decisions if parents and teachers keep them accountable for their actions.

Additionally, discipline aids in the development of self-control and self-discipline in children. Disciplined kids get better at controlling their emotions and behaviours, postponing gratification, and making appropriate decisions. Since children who can control their urges and concentrate on their studies typically perform better in school, this is crucial for academic achievement. Furthermore, because it enables people to overcome obstacles and accomplish their objectives, self-discipline is a crucial quality for success in life.

Additionally, discipline can aid in developing critical social skills in kids, like communication, empathy, and cooperation. Children who receive discipline learn how to behave politely and constructively among other people. Their social and emotional development may benefit greatly from the positive interactions they can form with peers, teachers, and other adults. Children can be better prepared for success in their jobs and in their personal lives if parents and educators teach them how to collaborate and communicate effectively.

Last but not least, children's emotional and psychological health depends on routine and structure, which discipline may give them. Discipline can help create a feeling of order and routine in children's lives as they flourish in predictable and consistent situations. Since it can give them a sense of security and stability, this might be particularly crucial for kids from chaotic or unstable homes.

The Balance Between Discipline and Kindness

Islam encourages parents to live up to the morals they want their children to learn. By continuously exhibiting integrity, tolerance, deference, and empathy, parents provide a concrete model for their kids to follow. This behaviour modelling is essential because it gives kids a practical example of how to behave in accordance with Islamic values. Children learn to emulate their parents when they witness them engaging in acts of worship, showing kindness to others, and showing patience in the face of adversity.

Islam advocates for a balanced approach to discipline, where firmness is tempered with compassion. Parents must neither be excessively strict nor overly lenient, as both extremes can adversely affect a child's development. A just balance ensures that discipline nurtures rather than harms, fostering respect, obedience, and love between parents and children. Prophet Muhammad (PBUH) exemplified this balance:

> *"The best among you are those who are best to their families" (Sunan Ibn Majah)*

This hadith emphasises that discipline should always be accompanied by kindness and respect, reinforcing the notion that correction should be done to nurture and improve, not merely punish.

The Quran also highlights the importance of balance in dealings with others, including children:

> *"And be moderate in your pace and lower your voice; indeed, the most disagreeable of sounds is the voice of donkeys" (Quran 31:19)*

This verse advises moderation, which extends to discipline—being neither too harsh nor too lax. A child disciplined with wisdom and love will develop into a well-rounded individual, capable of distinguishing right from wrong without feeling oppressed. The following are some fundamental ideas to keep in mind when you begin to think about raising your own children.

Be united: Regarding discipline, do you and your spouse agree? Show your children that you are one. Decide in advance how you and your partner will discipline your kids.

Discipline in private: Never give a public reprimand. Disciplining a child in a public setting is the most dehumanising and humiliating thing you can do to them. Inform them that they will receive discipline at home if they misbehave publicly. It's important you follow through with that.

Be dependable: You can have dozens of brilliant ideas and read every book in the world, but they won't work if you're not consistent. Maintaining consistency is difficult. Sometimes, letting your children get away with something is simpler than following through on your plan. But in the long term, consistency is rewarded. Our children benefit from knowing what to anticipate.

By following these rules and maintaining equilibrium, parents fulfil their duty of guiding their children while ensuring they grow up with a strong moral compass, emotional resilience, and a deep-rooted connection to their faith.

Implementing Effective Discipline Islamic Strategies

Discipline in Islam is deeply rooted in the teachings of the Quran and the Sunnah, emphasising fairness, consistency, and compassion. Effective Islamic discipline strategies revolve around setting clear boundaries, offering guidance rather than harsh punishment, and reinforcing positive behaviour through moral and ethical teachings.

The Prophet Muhammad (PBUH) demonstrated discipline with patience and wisdom, ensuring correction was done in a way that was nurtured rather than discouraged.

Practical Examples of Discipline That Align with Islamic Teachings

Practical discipline methods in Islam emphasise a balance between firmness and kindness. One effective example is using the power of storytelling. Parents and educators who want to inculcate Islamic principles in children's heads can benefit greatly from using Islamic moral stories for children. These tales, which are based on stories from the Quran and the lives of prophets, impart discipline, compassion, honesty, and perseverance in ways that kids can relate to and find interesting.

By telling their children these tales, parents help them develop a stronger bond with Islamic tradition and beliefs, giving them a sense of identity and purpose from a young age. In addition to teaching facts, these tales influence attitudes and actions consistent with Islamic values.

Islamic morals for children are based on the teachings of Islam and emphasise the values and precepts that direct behaviour and character formation. These values are crucial for helping kids develop a strong sense of morality, empathy, discipline and accountability.

Islamic stories teach kids discipline through inspiring lessons. Prophet Muhammad (PBUH) emphasised truthfulness, showing that honesty fosters responsibility. Prophet Ibrahim (AS) and Ismail (AS) demonstrated obedience to Allah and taught respect. Prophet Yusuf (AS) showed patience despite hardships, while the Quran's ants displayed hard work and teamwork.

Prophet Musa (AS) learned discipline through responsibility as a shepherd and leader. These lessons can be reinforced through storytelling, role-playing, and daily practice. Encouraging patience, honesty, and responsibility helps children develop strong character. Praise and rewards instil discipline, making Islamic teachings a practical guide for nurturing well-mannered and responsible children.

Another example is incorporating structured routines. Routines greatly benefit a child's growth and provide more than merely structure to daily life. They give kids a sense of security and predictability, which is essential for learning and development. Parents teach children improved self-management skills by creating consistent routines. This includes routines that teach accountability and time management from a young age, such as mealtimes, bedtimes, and school preparation.

Adhering to a regimen teaches children self-discipline. They learn to prioritise duties and maintain concentration on finishing them when they consistently follow planned activities and tasks. This self-disciplined habit encourages children to take responsibility for their activities and cultivate a sense of accountability.

It may be quite difficult to strike the correct balance when it comes to correcting our kids, especially if it's ongoing. But here's the thing: as kids become older and start to establish their independence, it's perfectly OK for them to challenge authority. But instead of using severe penalties that can undermine their self-worth and impede their emotional development, we want to point them in the correct direction.

Two distinct parenting philosophies that seek to influence a child's behaviour are positive discipline and punishment. Positive discipline aims to instruct and mentor kids using polite conversation and positive reinforcement. It places a strong emphasis on comprehending the fundamental causes of a child's behaviour and devising positive solutions.

To promote desirable behaviour, positive discipline entails establishing clear expectations, establishing consistent limits, and applying strategies, including rewards, problem-solving, encouragement, and reasonable punishments. It seeks to develop a solid bond between parents and children founded on respect, empathy, and trust.

Lastly, engaging in positive reinforcement—praising and rewarding good behaviour—aligns with Islamic values. The Prophet (PBUH) often encouraged good deeds through kind words and appreciation. Parents can follow this by acknowledging their children's efforts, boosting their confidence, and reinforcing the motivation to do well.

Encouraging Self-Discipline and Responsibility in Children

Self-discipline and responsibility are essential for a child's development and are deeply embedded in Islamic teachings. Islam encourages personal accountability and self-restraint, guiding children to develop these qualities early on. One effective method to instil self-discipline is teaching children the significance of prayer (Salah). Committing to praying on time fosters a sense of routine, responsibility, and devotion to Allah (SWT).

Another way to encourage self-discipline is through fasting during Ramadan. While young children are not obligated to fast, allowing them to observe partial fasts helps them understand self-control and patience. This practice gradually builds their ability to resist temptations and make conscious decisions aligned with Islamic values.

Parents can also cultivate responsibility by involving children in decision-making. Letting them choose their clothes, plan their study time, or participate in household chores instils a sense of accountability. Additionally, reinforcing the idea of honesty and integrity by explaining the concept of Amanah (trust) helps children grasp the importance of fulfilling obligations.

Another Islamic approach is teaching children delayed gratification. Encouraging them to save money for charity rather than spending impulsively teaches financial discipline and generosity. Through these practices, children develop self-discipline and responsibility, preparing them to lead principled and fulfilling lives in accordance with Islamic teachings.

Chapter Seven

Building Self-Esteem and Confidence

Nurturing a Positive Self-Image

While parents can't shield their kids from every difficult situation they encounter, we can teach them coping mechanisms. Common terms and concepts are used while discussing our children and our hopes for their future—especially as they mature and enter the workforce—terms like positive body image, self-assurance, and self-worth often come up.

However, as parents and caregivers, do we ever pause to truly reflect on these qualities, how they manifest, and how we can support our children in developing them? One of the most impactful things we can do daily is to help our children develop healthy and positive self-esteem.

How much a child values themselves and feels appreciated by others is a measure of their self-esteem. Over time, this sense of self-worth is cultivated and developed. Children with a solid sense of self-worth are often more inclined to try new things, more optimistic, and better able to face difficulties. To help children develop into well-adjusted individuals, this facet of their personalities must be fostered from a young age.

Children who have high self-esteem feel competent and self-assured. They respect their skills and themselves. They want to give it their all and are proud of their accomplishments. Children are more likely to have a growth attitude when they feel secure and confident about who they are. They can, therefore, inspire themselves to embark on new tasks. They can accept failure and grow from it.

Additionally, they're more inclined to advocate for themselves and seek assistance when necessary. As parents, we have an opportunity to help our kids develop a healthy sense of self. Let's see how!

Helping Children Develop a Healthy Sense of Self-worth

Children exhibit a need for respect and attention from an early age. They flaunt themselves to win admiration. They can occasionally resort to aggressive behaviours like fighting and screaming to attract and grab their parent's attention. Divergent opinions exist about the causes of this need for respect. According to religious academics, a divine soul exists within every human.

> *"So when I have made him complete and breathed into him of My spirit fall into prostration to him." (Quran 15:29)*

The magnificence and nobility of this divine spirit inspire everyone to strive for respect and dignity. He must be respected and would not inherently place himself in a disparaging or inferior role.

Morally and spiritually conscious kids grow up to feel good about themselves. One of the most crucial things parents can do for their children is to help them develop a strong sense of self-worth, which forms the basis of their faith and dedication to Allah (SWT). To give them worth, direction, and purpose in life, children must be reassured that they're a unique gift from Allah (SWT) and that they are to devote their abilities and resources to serving Him. Every stage of a child's growth requires moral and spiritual enrichment provisions, which inspire them to cherish their beauty and genuinely revere Allah (SWT).

High self-esteem or positive self-perceptions are best initiated at home, and we must instil this in our children from infancy. Our parents' or guardians' opinions of us are the main source of gratitude for who Allah (SWT) has created us to be. Children judge themselves against the norms set by those influencing their lives, mirroring how others see them. A child requires our undivided affection.

Even if we express disapproval of inappropriate behaviour, children still want to feel valued. Our unwavering love for our kids will strengthen and uplift their belief in Allah (SWT) and inculcate the belief that "I am lovable, I am confident." People with a good sense of self-worth can better make decisions, show gratitude for their achievements, accept responsibility, and handle stressful situations more effectively.

Many people, after recognising the importance of self-esteem in a child's life, wonder what can be done to nurture it. There are numerous things parents may do—or not do—to help their children learn self-respect.

The following advice is not meant to create arrogance or entitlement but rather to foster a healthy sense of self-worth. When applied in moderation, these strategies can help children build confidence without becoming overindulged or spoiled.

This is what we can do as parents:

Encourage Our Children to Take Action

A newborn feels a sense of comprehension and joy as they learn to hold a cup or take their first steps. Things like learning to read, dress, or ride a bike are opportunities for a child's self-esteem to develop as they get older. Similarly, children learn that difficulties are a natural part of life but that there is always hope and relief after adversity when they're taught the strength of faith and dependence on Allah (SWT). Their faith is strengthened, and their self-esteem is increased by promoting frequent prayer, learning, and worship.

Start by demonstrating and offering assistance. Then, even if children make mistakes, let them accomplish what they can. This is essential to cultivating a healthy sense of self-worth. Give your children the opportunity to study, attempt, and feel proud. Avoid making new tasks too simple or too complex. Tell them they don't have to be flawless; encourage them to always try their hardest.

Respect Them

Respecting children is not something that many parents believe is required. While they expect respect in return, they feel that showing their child respect would be akin to indulging them. Nonetheless, showing your children respect in the following ways will make them feel good about themselves and appreciate you more voluntarily:

Encourage your child to express their thoughts whenever they want to, and never make fun of or belittle them. While a child lacks the same maturity as an adult, they nevertheless deserve to be heard. Dismissing their thoughts as unimportant is one of the best ways to stifle their creativity and thoughtful expression.

Some parents think it's useless to communicate with their children since they can't comprehend at the same level as adults. However, children who receive more conversation tend to grow up to be more perceptive and understanding than those who do not. These children know their parents think highly of them and feel they can communicate with them. It's a huge confidence boost.

When speaking to others, speak highly of them. Children feel genuine appreciation when they hear positive comments about themselves. There's no need for excessive or unwarranted praise, but when your child does something well, share it with friends, family, or others.

This approach will seem more sincere and have a greater impact than offering direct praise. Any sense of self-worth a child may have is frequently destroyed by parents who publicly criticise and moan about them in front of them.

Don't completely ruin your child's sense of self-worth when you reprimand them. Instead of giving them a broad "you are good for nothing" attitude, which, if repeated frequently, may cause the child to truly believe it, reprimand them for specific behaviour. Even while parents are quick to point out bad behaviour, they should keep in mind the positive traits their children possess.

Give Credit When Credit is Due

Refrain from praising attributes like intelligence or athleticism or results like receiving an A. Instead, commend your child for their attitude, effort, and progress. For instance: "You're doing well on that project," "You're getting better at these spelling tests," or "I'm proud of you for offering prayers on time" Kids attempt, work towards goals, and put effort into things when they receive this kind of praise and have a higher chance of success as a result.

Take note of your children's strengths and interests. Make sure they have chances to develop these things. To make someone feel good about them, emphasise their strengths more than their shortcomings.

Tell Them Tales of Admirable Individuals

Children adore stories, making them a powerful tool in teaching important concepts. Take the opportunity to share motivational tales of admirable individuals with young children. Muslim parents, in particular, can benefit from the many Islamic children's books available today.

Children are frequently influenced by heroes and their noble deeds, which can encourage them to act honourably rather than lectures from parents.

Encourage Them to Have Healthy Friendships.

Children should be taught that their best friends are those who treat them with respect and encourage them via their actions and words. Teach them that they should avoid those who act in a way that belittles others. They should instead pick people who support them in being themselves and with whom they can be themselves. Assist them in being that kind of friend to others.

Children's self-esteem rises when they realise that their actions impact other people. They can do a favour for a sibling, assist at home, or complete a project at school. Self-esteem and other positive emotions are increased when one helps others and performs deeds of kindness.

Instil Them With a Sense of Self-worth

Urge your children to have high standards for themselves and work toward meaningful goals. Help them succeed and reach the best of their ability in school, the madrasah, and any extra activities they're passionate about. A parent's attention and encouragement inspire the child to try hard in everyday activities. Show them that some things, such as excessive whining, constantly requesting stuff from other people, or breaking the law, are beneath their dignity. By promoting this mindset, they'll become accustomed to a particular behaviour.

Promoting Confidence through Positive Experiences

Many parents worry about raising self-assured and socially proficient children, particularly when their children behave shyly around others. Being shy is merely one aspect of being bashful. While shyness can be a normal and occasionally advantageous quality, it frequently manifests as an inability to fit in and communicate with people. Shy children may seem timid, reticent, and hesitant to engage with their classmates, especially in new or social situations. If not addressed, shyness can have enduring effects on a child's social and emotional development, unlike other forms of shyness that may eventually be outgrown.

This conduct is frequently the result of low self-esteem, embarrassment anxiety, or the promotion of stillness as a virtue. If children receive praise for being silent or staying out of trouble, they may become even more reclusive and avoid any interactions that can make them uncomfortable.

Confidence is a talent that can be developed via deliberate experiences rather than an innate quality. Children's perceptions of themselves and their skills are greatly influenced by positive experiences. It takes time, empathy, and a consistent strategy to help a shy child gain confidence and social skills. The following are some methods to help your child:

Creating Opportunities

Although being a parent is one of the hardest jobs in the world, there is no official training on effective parenting techniques. The good news is that parents can use everyday experiences as extraordinary learning opportunities and stimulate their children's brains in a variety of ways.

Every event in a kid's life is an opportunity to learn. Bath time, laundry sorting, cooking, and running errands are all excellent learning opportunities. Explain your language-stimulating activities. Play with ingredients and textures to encourage scientific thinking, and count and sort laundry to teach numeracy. One of the best ways to teach emotional intelligence is to make faces representing various emotions.

> *"We shall certainly test you with fear and hunger, and loss of property, lives, and crops, But [Prophet], give good news to those who are steadfast, those who say when afflicted with a calamity, 'We belong to God and to Him we shall return.' These will be given blessings and mercy from their Lord, and it's they who are rightly guided." (Quran 2:155-157)*

In this ayah, "steadfast" is the essential word. What does being steadfast mean? It implies "to be resolutely or dutifully firm and unwavering," according to the dictionary. Because it's a quality Allah (SWT) would like to see in His creation when we work to develop ourselves and the world for His sake, this word is frequently employed throughout the Quran. It's not a characteristic that we are born with, though. Throughout our lives, we're supposed to cultivate and improve it until we arrive at Paradise, the prize of the Hereafter.

As parents, instilling steadfastness in our children becomes crucial to their upbringing. By demonstrating resilience and unwavering faith in our daily lives, we provide them with real-life examples of how to navigate challenges with patience and trust in Allah (SWT). Teaching them the value of perseverance and faith-based decision-making fosters a mindset that prepares them to face difficulties with strength and wisdom. Ultimately, this nurtures an environment where parents and children grow together, creating continuous learning and spiritual development opportunities.

A growth mindset is the belief that one's abilities may be enhanced by diligence, wise tactics, and feedback from others. A person with a "fixed mindset," on the other hand, feels that their abilities are natural gifts that they possess from birth. Children with a growth attitude consistently performed better.

Alongside the frustration children will experience when learning a skill, participating in a sport, or engaging in any other activity, parents should provide encouragement that emphasises the time and effort their children are investing in the skill rather than how "good or bad" they are at it. To acquire that skill and accomplish their goal, parents should help their children understand why they're feeling anxious, depressed, or frustrated. This understanding drastically alters their workflow and helps them hone their abilities as they become more adept at getting back up after falling or encountering obstacles.

As you cultivate a growth attitude in your kids, you must also model it for them. Do your best to communicate with them constructively, offering only carefully considered constructive criticism. Establish a growth mindset atmosphere that encourages inquiry and discovery. Give them the chance to work together, exchange ideas, and learn from their classmates.

Honour their accomplishments and efforts, fostering an encouraging and supportive environment where they feel free to take chances, make errors, and develop. Children who accept obstacles and failures as teaching moments are resilient, adept at overcoming problems, and driven to improve.

Children have a sponge-like mentality. Without conscious effort, it has a propensity to take in whatever stimuli and information it encounters. Because children will absorb everything at an incredible velocity that will influence their development, it's crucial to guide them in the information they are exposed to throughout their early years.

Children are exposed to information throughout these years for the rest of their lives, ranging from social, linguistic, and physical abilities to knowledge of the deen (Islam) and comprehension of their surroundings. They will continue to draw upon this foundational knowledge throughout their lives.

Make an effort to teach them Islam since, as Muslims, staying on the straight path that Allah (SWT) has directed is the key to our prosperity. The most important resource for our future is our children, who are the result of our culture. As adults, we have a big say in how a child feels and acts. We possess the ability to inspire and encourage them. Learning about our deen must be portrayed in a pleasant light. Setting a good example is the only way to accomplish this.

If you don't try to do the same as your child, you'll have very little influence over their desire to study. Making learning about the deen enjoyable, engaging, and requiring work are the keys to inspiring your child to learn about it.

Consider the question, "Why am I doing this?" We must always choose to act for the benefit of Allah (SWT). Insha'Allah, this will reward you and help you maintain concentration. Write down specific things you want your child to learn. Try to be as specific as possible; the more detailed, the better.

The goal is to assist, not overwhelm. If there are subjects you believe you lack enough understanding of, take this as inspiration to learn more about them first. Seek assistance from others; this will give everyone the chance to benefit. Make a plan for how you'll discuss the particular subjects over the month. Yes, push yourself, but remember that you can't possibly finish everything in a single month.

Make it enjoyable by using games. For instance, if your child is being taught to memorise some of the 99 Names of Allah, they'll more likely retain and learn the material if they actively participate in it. When teaching a certain subject, use a range of activities. Since everyone learns differently, take note of this in your planning.

Involve other family members by inviting them over. But remember that if you don't follow through on your strategy, it will only end up being a social event, and you won't have accomplished your objective.

Money or ostentatious educational materials have nothing to do with providing your child with the best resources for success in the future. It's all about you, your time, and how involved you are.

Chapter Eight

Teaching Gratitude and Contentment

Instilling the Value of Shukr (Gratitude)

Despite being one of the most potent forms of prayer in Islam, Shukr, or gratitude, is sometimes overlooked and forgotten in the chaos and bustle of everyday life. We frequently fail to stand back and show gratitude for the innumerable gifts that Allah (SWT) has so kindly bestowed upon us as our minds are consumed by our problems, goals, and wants.

Despite what many people think, being grateful is much more than just saying "Alhamdulillah." It's a way of thinking, a continuous practice, and a transformational force that shapes how we view the world, other people, and our relationship with Allah (SWT).

In Islam, Shukr is a seemingly insignificant but really important idea that Allah (SWT) has brought up numerous times in the Holy Quran.

> *"And ˹remember˺ when your Lord proclaimed, 'If you are grateful, I will certainly give you more. But if you are ungrateful, surely My punishment is severe." (Quran 14:7)*

In Islam, gratitude is a way to glorify Allah (SWT). The Prophet Muhammad (PBUH) served as an example of this throughout his life, particularly when he offered night prayers. Despite possessing a high spiritual rank, he would spend several hours in prayer.

> *When questioned why he prayed so fervently, he responded: "Shall I not be a grateful servant?" (Sahih Bukhari)*

This proves that showing gratitude is more than just saying "thank you"; it also entails doing it by worshipping, praising, and obeying Allah (SWT).

Personal development and spiritual purification are also associated with gratitude. An appreciative person has greater inner peace, cultivates a good view of life, and deepens their relationship with Allah (SWT).

The teachings of Hadith show that Shukr is both a duty and a means of achieving happiness, mental well-being, and spiritual elevation. Thus, the teachings of Islam that emphasise thankfulness greatly influence how Muslims see Allah (SWT), other people, and themselves.

Being thankful enhances one's spiritual life, brings one closer to Allah (SWT), and promotes kindness and humility in daily life.

Your child can adopt a more positive approach and alter their perspective when confronted with a difficult circumstance if they cultivate an "attitude of gratitude." There are a few main ways in which we can divide the various ways we can thank Allah (SWT). Let's have a look at these:

Teaching Children to Appreciate and Be Thankful for Allah's (SWT) Blessings

Here are a few doable strategies to help you incorporate Islamic teachings while raising appreciative kids:

Assist them in understanding its significance: Children may recognise this expression from their interactions with adults, but they must realise that it's a lovely prayer for the person you wish to show your appreciation for, rather than merely the Arabic equivalent of saying "thank you." It'll also help instil the idea that Allah's (SWT) bounties and gifts are far greater than anything we could possibly offer on this planet.

If they comprehend its meaning, they might find it simpler to use this statement as a token of gratitude. Saying the sentence in English or the child's native tongue has the same impact and meaning, even if they are unable to speak it in Arabic. The aim is to get kids to understand the meaning of the words rather than just saying them at the appropriate times.

Use strategies to help them comprehend and retain the term's meaning: This could involve narrating stories, making flashcards, or writing a little poem or rhyme.

Share anecdotes from the Quran—like the one about Prophet Ayoub (AS)—that inspire us to be thankful to Allah (SWT).

Lead by example: Children pick up a lot of knowledge from watching their parents. Your child is likely to follow suit if you show thankfulness frequently. In front of your children, make it a habit to repeat "Alhamdulillah" (All praise is due to Allah) both during prayer and in daily situations. Expressing thanks in words and deeds, such as thanking Allah (SWT) for a lovely day, a delicious meal, or a safe trip, teaches kids the value of thankfulness. As parents, we may teach our kids a valuable lesson by modelling an attitude of thankfulness.

Make time for nature: We might feel more thankful to Allah (SWT) when we spend time in nature. Awe-inspiring experiences include observing the clouds, taking in sunsets with others, identifying patterns on leaves, and marvelling at the height of the trees and the grandeur of the mountains. Making time for nature a priority and allowing our children to participate in appreciating and connecting the beauty of our planet to its creator would help them recognise Allah's (SWT) boundless blessings and experience thankfulness.

Maintain reasonable, age-appropriate expectations: It's crucial to acknowledge that children will naturally have limitations when experiencing and expressing appreciation. Additionally, when our children express strong feelings like sadness, rage, or frustration, we must be careful not to use words like "be grateful" or "don't complain" as an excuse to shut them down.

On the other hand, it's highly improbable that telling somebody to "be grateful" when they are upset will make them feel thankful. If we create room for their sentiments, connect with them, and meet them where they are, it will be quite easy for them to be open to our attempts to establish a personal relationship with Allah (SWT) and feel thankful.

Encourage them to be charitable: It's crucial to keep in mind that cultivating appreciation towards Allah (SWT) involves more than just feeling thankful; it also involves our deeds. This is especially true when we're trying to instil feelings of thankfulness in our children. Among the fundamental ways we can put our thankfulness into practice are through our daily prayers and charitable contributions to the community and the impoverished. By involving our children in social welfare initiatives and encouraging them to share their talents with others, we intentionally support our children.

Urge them to engage in community work, donate clothing, or share toys. In addition to fostering empathy, these activities teach kids to be grateful for what they have. Giving to people in need is strongly encouraged in Islam, and instilling this concept at a young age can have a long-lasting effect. Your child can learn that performing charitable deeds, or "sadaqah," is a way to thank Allah (SWT) for all of the benefits He has given us.

Raising appreciative kids requires teaching them to say "thank you" when someone gives them something or helps them. Encourage them to express their gratitude orally or in writing. From this small deed, they learn to value those around them and to appreciate the goodwill of others. In Islam, giving thanks to others is a means of giving thanks to Allah (SWT); as the Prophet Muhammad (PBUH) said:

> *"He who does not thank people, does not thank Allah."*
> *(Ahmad, Tirmidhi)*

Reflecting on the Quran: Another important way to thank Allah (SWT) is by reading the Quran and thinking about it. Allah (SWT) has given us the Quran, which serves as a source of wisdom to assist Muslims in dealing with the difficulties of life. Additionally, it's a means of communication that strengthens the believer's spiritual bond with his Lord.

By reading the Quran and considering its passages, we can better understand Allah (SWT), His expectations of us, and how to express our thankfulness. We can also consider Allah's (SWT) manifestations in the world and ourselves. Gratitude results from this introspection, which increases one's appreciation for Allah's (SWT) blessings.

Whether your child is two, five, or thirteen years old, if you haven't already, start today. Although it's best to change your habits or behaviours as soon as possible, it's never too late to change theirs as well. As children grow older, it may take a little longer, but as long as you remain consistent and conscientious in your actions, it's still very possible, insha'Allah. The process of raising appreciative children is ongoing and requires perseverance and patience. Insha'Allah, begin cultivating thankfulness in your children now and observe them develop into appreciative, kind, and happy adults.

Promoting Contentment and Avoiding Materialism

Contentment (rida or qana'a in Arabic) is the right attitude towards things we don't have, but gratitude is the right attitude towards the gifts we have received. To be content is surrendering to Allah's (SWT) will and accepting what He has provided us.

One essential component of soul purification is contentment. Without it, greed can take over and, regardless of our accomplishments, leave us feeling always unsatisfied. Many hadiths caution us against the perils of greed and remind us of the benefits of contentment.

> *The Prophet (PBUH) said: "Wealth is not in having many possessions. Rather, true wealth is the richness of the soul." (Sahih Bukhari)*

> *He (PBUH) also said, "Whoever among you wakes up secure in his property, healthy in his body, and with his food for the day, it is as if he were given the entire world." (Tirmidhi)*

After working hard and giving our all, we should be satisfied with whatever Allah (SWT) has given us for the day. Contentment comes after striving. Islam encourages us to strive for excellence in all facets of our lives, including our careers, financial situation, and relationships with our families.

We should endeavour to be the finest versions of ourselves, putting in great effort to achieve admirable and significant objectives. But this effort should be followed by contentment—being happy with a hard day's work, even if the outcomes aren't what we had hoped for. Being pleased even when we don't accomplish all of our goals is what it means to be content.

Islam, however, forbids individuals from losing themselves in worldly pursuits and neglecting God and the afterlife. In reality, a person must maintain balance in all aspects of life, fulfilling the rights of Allah (SWT), themselves, and others without sacrificing one duty to satisfy another.

Let's explore how we can educate our children about these two concepts as Muslim parents:

Encouraging a Sense of Contentment and Satisfaction with What They Have

Setting a positive example: When parents demonstrate gratitude and satisfaction with what they have, children naturally adopt the same mindset. Expressing thanks for both big and small blessings reinforces the idea that happiness doesn't depend on accumulating material wealth.

Emphasise experiences over possessions: Encouraging children to appreciate family time, friendships, and simple joys helps shift their focus from material desires to meaningful connections. Teaching them about the concept of barakah (divine blessing) also reinforces that true fulfilment comes from appreciating what is already present in their lives.

Limit unnecessary exposure to excessive consumerism: In today's digital world, advertisements and social media often fuel materialistic desires. Parents can counter this by encouraging discussions about the difference between needs and wants, helping children develop a balanced perspective. Engaging in charitable acts also fosters contentment by demonstrating to children the importance of giving rather than constantly seeking more.

Encouraging gratitude as a daily habit: Simple routines, such as sharing what they are thankful for each day, can create a mindset of appreciation. Additionally, involving them in household responsibilities teaches the value of effort and earning rewards, reinforcing the principle that contentment follows sincere effort.

Addressing the Negative Effects of Materialism and How to Counter Them

Materialism often leads to dissatisfaction, entitlement, and an endless pursuit of more. When children associate happiness with acquiring new things, they become less appreciative of what they already have. Over time, this mindset fosters impatience, unrealistic expectations, and an inability to find joy in non-material aspects of life.

One way to counteract materialism is by instilling a strong sense of purpose beyond possessions. Encouraging children to develop hobbies, engage in community service, and pursue knowledge helps shift their focus from ownership to self-improvement and meaningful contributions.

As parents, you should also be mindful of your own spending habits, as children learn from observing adult behaviour. When parents prioritise mindful spending and delayed gratification, children internalise the importance of financial responsibility.

Another crucial step is to limit excessive exposure to advertisements and consumer-driven entertainment. Instead of allowing marketing messages to dictate their desires, children should be encouraged to find fulfilment in creativity, relationships, and faith. By cultivating a mindset of gratitude, moderation, and self-awareness mindset, they can grow into individuals who value inner richness over external possessions.

Chapter Nine

Encouraging Healthy Relationships and Social Skills

Fostering Positive Social Interactions

Good interactions are essential to children's and adolescents' healthy development. Building healthy relationships in the early, formative years is essential for the development of social skills and emotional control because it creates the supportive atmosphere needed for these abilities to thrive.

A strong sense of self-worth, feelings for others, and resilience are often developed in children and young adults with stable, caring, and supportive connections with their parents, guardians, teachers, classmates, and mentors.

These relationships provide a secure environment in which they can learn how to resolve conflicts, examine their feelings, and hone their communication abilities. Positive relationships also help people feel connected and at home, which is important for emotional health and the formation of a strong moral compass.

Essentially, during the critical phases of childhood and adolescence, these relationships act as the foundation for normal emotional, social, and behavioural development.

Thus, interactions between individuals and their surroundings lead to the process of development. Social connection is very important for children's growth. For this reason, parents and other carers must provide their children with lots of chances to socialise.

Teaching Children to Build and Maintain Healthy Friendships

Friends are like flowers. You want to keep some of them close at hand since they smell and look nice. Some are aesthetically pleasing even though they have no scent at all. Others have thorns that, if not handled carefully, can cause pain.

Some flowers need considerable care but may bring a lot of goodness into your life, while others are simple to maintain and will bloom year after year with little work. You will always select the finest bouquet of flowers to adorn your house. Similarly, we should constantly choose the greatest friends—those who will help us and serve as a reminder of Allah (SWT).

Friends have various demands and come in a variety of colours, shapes, and sizes, just like flowers. They do, however, share certain characteristics, such as the requirement for soil, water, and sunlight, or whatever else keeps them alive. A functional community is a site that offers the elements and shelter a flower needs to grow, and relationships flourish there.

This community's planting bed has to have rich soil and lots of room for different kinds of vegetation. Consider yourself a flower or a lovely plant that benefits other people. You're an aroma that appeals to the senses, embodying gentleness, sustenance, beauty, and shade. Your lovely, smiling face, which is like vibrant petals in full bloom, makes people feel at ease and welcome.

Having good friends who are devoted to one's faith can strengthen one's own religion and result in great spiritual growth. Conversely, forming friendships with individuals who practise immorality or possess weak faith may expose one to harmful influences and potentially divert one from the straight and narrow.

Islam advises us to choose friends who are kind, caring, honest, trustworthy, and of high character. These individuals are like sweet-smelling flowers or perfume vendors.

These attributes support a healthy and constructive social environment and aid in our own growth. In Islam, selecting close friends is crucial. They can support us in upholding our religious ideals and ideas, which can have a positive effect on our religion. By teaching children Islamic values and principles from an early age and modelling good behaviour, we can help our children make wise friendship choices.

Making excellent friends is very important in Islam since the people we spend time with can greatly influence our beliefs, behaviour, and deeds.

> *"A man is upon the religion of his best friend, so let one of you look at whom he befriends." (Tirmidhi)*

As parents, we should promote open communication with our children to create an atmosphere where they feel comfortable discussing their social lives with us. This will enable us to constructively address any worries or problems our children may have with their friends.

It starts with compassion (show empathy or "put yourself in their shoes"), patience (let them express themselves without interfering), and affection (offer them love). Communicating with our children in this way will undoubtedly keep the lines of communication open.

> *Abu Huraira reported that Al-Aqra ibn Habis saw the Prophet kissing his grandson, Hasan (RA). He then said to him: I have ten children, but I have never kissed any one of them," after which the Prophet responded: 'He who does not show mercy (toward his children), no mercy would be shown to him.'" (Sahih Muslim)*

By inviting them over for get-togethers, going to Islamic events with them, and participating in character-building activities, we can help our kids make friends. Children require socialisation and a sense of belonging, just like adults do. Getting together with their pals can help them decompress and give them chances to do more nice deeds.

As parents, we must keep an eye on our children's friendships and get to know their friends and families. By doing this, we can detect any negative influences and ensure they're interacting with the right people.

Modelling and Encouraging Respectful and Kind Behaviour

Positive activities like volunteering, helping others, and attending Islamic events and gatherings are things that we can urge our children to do. This will provide your children the opportunity to interact with people who share their views. They'll also develop empathy for others and emotional awareness—two abilities that will help them later in life.

The Prophet (PBUH) gave his people numerous examples of how Muslims should treat one another.

> *At one point, he stated: "The parable of the believers in their affection, mercy, and compassion for each other is that of a body. When any limb aches, the whole body reacts with sleeplessness and fever." (Sahih Bukhari)*

Good friends from all ethnicities and backgrounds are welcome. When their child's social circle grows to include individuals from different cultural backgrounds, some Muslim parents start to worry. For instance, they're concerned that their son or daughter may be a negative influence if they make friends with a non-Muslim.

Nevertheless, these anxieties frequently stem from unjust prejudices, ignorance, or even racism. In actuality, these connections are crucial for exposing children to people from diverse backgrounds.

Regardless of their faith or beliefs, Muslims are taught by Islam to treat everyone with kindness, respect, and justice. Muslims are urged to keep positive connections with their neighbours, coworkers, children, and others regardless of their religion or culture. Every non-Muslim can be an ally or Muslim. Since no one is certain to die a believer, we should learn to view others as we see ourselves.

Throughout his life, the Prophet Muhammad (PBUH) mingled with individuals of many faiths and gave them compassion regardless of their views.

It's our duty as Muslims to be good friends and to pick our friends carefully. By adhering to the important teachings in the Quran and the Sunnah about seeking out uplifting and encouraging friendships, we may assist our children in developing solid and meaningful relationships that enhance their lives and help them become better Muslims and better people.

Handling Peer Pressure and Social Challenges

Peer relationships can become increasingly important as kids get older. Peer pressure can force some children to do things they may not feel safe doing or to act in a particular way. Peer pressure is a strong factor affecting kids' behaviour in any situation. Recognise that peer pressure has advantages even if many parents and educators are aware of its detrimental impacts.

Encouraging their peers to put in extra effort and perform well in their studies is one of the most prevalent examples of positive peer pressure among children. When children observe their peers striving for excellence, they may feel inspired to work harder. They can motivate one another to produce their best work, thus creating a positive feedback loop. Furthermore, children may inspire their peers to take on leadership roles or participate in extracurricular activities. As a result, they may develop a stronger sense of connection and be encouraged to explore new interests and skills.

However, negative peer pressure can be harmful. Children might, for instance, urge their peers to partake in detrimental activities such as drug and alcohol misuse, skipping school, or cheating on tests. Children trying to establish their social identity or fit in may find this kind of pressure particularly difficult. Youngsters who feel compelled to conform may resort to these risky behaviours to avoid rejection or exclusion.

Peer pressure is a complicated phenomenon that can influence kids' behaviour in both positive and bad ways. Bad peer pressure can result in dangerous behaviours, bullying, and unfavourable consequences, whereas positive peer pressure can motivate kids to put in extra effort and do their best. As parents and educators, it's important to recognise the many types of peer pressure,

Children who learn how to deal with peer pressure are better equipped to make decisions independently, become resilient, and have positive self-esteem. This ability is crucial because it enables individuals to remain loyal to who they truly are and make decisions consistent with their values and goals.

Guiding Children in Dealing with Peer Pressure and Making Ethical Choices

Here are a few strategies to assist your children overcome the negative effects of peer pressure.

Pay Attention to Your Child

It's among the most crucial actions parents can take. Make time for your child and offer them your undivided attention when they approach you to communicate. Even if they say something that makes you angry, don't interrupt them. The goal is to create a safe haven for them. If they feel like they're unable to communicate with you, they'll likely avoid future talks.

Telling your child, "I hear what you said to me, and I am glad that you came to me, but I want a few minutes to reflect on which is the most appropriate to respond to you or the best way to help you," is fine if you need some time to gather your thoughts. The most important thing is to return to your child with advice or guidance.

Encourage Them to Critically Think

If you teach your child to think critically, they can make judgements based on logic, reason, and an awareness of consequences. Instead of taking things at face value, encourage them to think critically and ask questions. One method of fostering critical thinking is asking open-ended questions that motivate them to think about various points of view and possible outcomes.

For instance, when talking about a peer's recommendation, ask them, "What do you believe might happen if you follow this advice? In what ways does it correspond with your personal values and beliefs?" By doing this, they are prompted to consider the long-term effects of their decisions and look beyond the here and now by these and related concerns. Their ability to make decisions enables them to evaluate their options, think through the repercussions, and then make wise decisions consistent with their beliefs and ideals.

Help Them Identify Their Values

Children who receive assistance in defining their values can better envision what they stand for and will be more capable of making decisions consistent with their principles. Start by having candid discussions about values and their importance. You can ask them, "What is the most essential thing to you?"

As your child's values become more apparent to them, assist them in realising how these values might influence their choices. Urge them to consider how crucial it's to uphold their morals even in the face of difficulty. As individuals grow more confident in their identity and convictions, this process allows them to make better decisions and increases their self-confidence.

Teach Them How to Say "No."

Role-play various situations with them and practise your rejection techniques. Tell them that going against the crowd or resisting peer pressure will sometimes be challenging. That being said, they must be ready to know what to say or do. Have them come up with a code phrase or sentence that they can use in an emergency. For instance, saying, "I want pizza for dinner tonight," may indicate that your child feels unsafe or that you must pick them up immediately.

Establish and Uphold Clear Family Rules

Make sure your child is aware of any family customs that hold special meaning for you. Some families make it a point to have supper together every day, and everyone is expected to be present. Establish and adhere to clear guidelines for screen or gadget time. Assign age-appropriate tasks to encourage accountability. Stress your family's beliefs and try to create a safe and secure atmosphere for your child.

Develop Self-Esteem

Children who feel good about themselves are more likely to make choices that are consistent with their own values and views and are less prone to seek approval from their peers. However, peer pressure can negatively affect a child's self-esteem, so it's critical to discover strategies to continuously boost self-worth and confidence.

Praising and encouraging children for their efforts and accomplishments, however minor, can increase their confidence. Supporting their interests and hobbies is another method to promote self-esteem. Children's confidence is boosted when they succeed in subjects they are enthusiastic about. By fostering an atmosphere that celebrates their individuality and strengths, we assist them in developing a solid sense of self-worth, which enables them to fend off harmful peer pressure.

Improve Social Skills and Deal with Bullying

Children can gain independence and the ability to make friends, speak well, and resolve disagreements constructively. These abilities can give children more self-assurance and independence when navigating social settings.

Bullying is a sort of peer pressure that can occasionally be dangerous and emotionally harmful. Children can learn from their parents how to deal with bullying by speaking up, asking for adult assistance, and defending others being harassed.

Help and Encourage Good Friend Selection

Urge your children to be careful who they associate with. Discuss what makes good companions: someone who respects them, shares their beliefs and encourages them to grow. Stress how crucial it's that they surround themselves with friends who encourage and uplift them rather than ones who could steer them in the wrong direction.

Encourage your children to participate in groups and activities that reflect their values and interests, as this can inevitably result in the development of wholesome friendships. Be willing to meet and get to know their friends, and if you think a friend might be a bad influence, don't be scared to voice your worries or observations. By doing this, you're assisting them in creating a solid support system that will enable them to defy peer pressure and make morally sound decisions.

Future relationships and deeper connections are made possible by the capacity to resist peer pressure. It involves developing a strong sense of self-awareness and personal ideals and fending off harmful influences. It teaches children how important it is to surround themselves with peers who value their development and respect their boundaries.

By teaching our children how to handle peer pressure, we provide them with the skills to live happy, meaningful lives and develop into strong, self-assured adults who can defend their values against outside pressure.

Chapter Ten

Managing Stress and Mental Health

Recognising Signs of Stress and Anxiety

Every child and adolescent experiences stress occasionally. Stress is a common reaction to difficulties and transitions. And even as a child, life is full of those. Any situation where a child must adjust or change might cause childhood stress. Although stress can be brought on by positive changes like starting a new hobby, it is most frequently associated with negative events like a family member's illness or death.

Stress can affect children in ways comparable to those experienced by adults. They experience bodily alterations and increased psychological and emotional susceptibility when under stress. A stress response system is triggered in children's brains when they experience stress due to environmental factors. Stress hormones are released into their systems, raising their degree of arousal and causing their blood pressure and pulse rate to increase. Even if your child doesn't seem particularly stressed out on the surface, this can occur on the inside.

Small, temporary stressors, like the pressure of a school deadline, are acceptable and can inspire kids to act. However, it has been demonstrated that chronic, daily, and persistent activation of a child's stress response system can alter the brain's growing architecture and negatively impact their general development and well-being, particularly if the stress is uncontrollable.

Stress is a transient reaction to a difficult or dangerous circumstance, while anxiety is a chronic emotional state. Even when there isn't a clear explanation, these emotions can get in the way of day-to-day activity. It's critical to comprehend these distinctions.

Identifying Symptoms of Stress in Children

Children experience stress differently than adults, and their reactions may manifest through behavioural, emotional, and physical symptoms. Some common signs of stress in children include:

- Frequent headaches or stomachaches without a medical explanation.
- Sleep disturbances, such as insomnia or nightmares.
- Changes in appetite—either excessive eating or loss of appetite.
- Irritability, mood swings, or frequent emotional outbursts.
- Difficulty concentrating or declining academic performance.
- Withdrawal from family, friends, or social activities.
- Unexplained fears or increased anxiety.

Islam teaches that stress and anxiety are natural aspects of life but should be managed with trust in Allah and proper coping mechanisms. The Quran reassures believers:

> *"And We will surely test you with something of fear and hunger and a loss of wealth and lives and fruits, but give good tidings to the patient" (Quran 2:155)*

This verse reminds us that trials and hardships are part of life, and patience is key to overcoming them.

Providing Support and Intervention When Needed

Once stress symptoms are identified in children, parents and guardians must provide support and necessary intervention. Some effective strategies include:

- **Open Communication:** Encouraging children to express their feelings without fear of judgment.

- **Providing Reassurance**: Reminding them that stress is temporary and that Allah's help is always near.

- **Creating a Routine:** Maintaining a stable daily routine to reduce uncertainty and anxiety.

- **Limiting Exposure to Stressors**: Reducing academic or social pressure when necessary.

- **Seeking Professional Help**: Consulting Islamic scholars or mental health professionals when stress becomes overwhelming.

> *The Prophet Muhammad (PBUH) emphasised the importance of mental well-being and emotional support, stating: "The strong believer is better and more beloved to Allah than the weak believer, but there is good in both. Strive for what benefits you, seek help from Allah, and do not give up" (Sahih Muslim)*

This hadith teaches that while we should work towards strength, seeking help and remaining steadfast in faith is also important.

Implementing Coping Strategies

Islam provides a comprehensive framework for managing stress and maintaining mental health. Implementing Islamic-based coping strategies helps individuals build resilience and find inner peace.

Teaching Stress Management Techniques Based on Islamic Practices

Islam encourages believers to manage stress through various spiritual and practical approaches, including:

Connecting with Allah (SWT)

Trusting Allah alleviates stress. The Quran states,

> *"And whoever relies upon Allah—then He is sufficient for him" (Quran 65:3)*

Regularly seeking forgiveness cleanses the heart and reduces the burden of guilt or stress. Establishing daily prayers provides spiritual comfort and reduces anxiety.

> *Allah (SWT) says, "Verily, in the remembrance of Allah do hearts find rest" (Quran 13:28)*

As Muslims, we must pray five times a day (Salah). This can be a very effective way to manage stress and encourage mindfulness (Muraqabah). You can develop a stronger sense of awareness and presence throughout each prayer by pausing for a few moments to consider your feelings and thoughts. When you're feeling stressed or anxious, this can help you remain composed and focused.

Reciting the Quran

Reading the Quran brings tranquillity. For believers, the Quran is a heavenly guide that illuminates the way and aids in navigating life's challenges. It gives life meaning and purpose by fostering a closer relationship with Allah (SWT) and offering spiritual guidance. The Quran guides people to the light of truth from the darkness of ignorance. Its lessons are essential for success in this life and finding salvation in the next.

> *As stated by Allah (SWT) in the Quran: "Surely this Quran guides to what is most upright and gives good news to the believers—who do good—that they will have a mighty reward." (Quran 17:9)*

Children's cognitive abilities are enhanced when they learn to read the Quran. Students attempting to comprehend difficult ideas in their verses improves their capacity for memory, focus, and critical thought. Children learn patience, gratitude, and contentment with what they have from the Quran. Additionally, it offers consolation and support at trying times, fostering a positive outlook on life and emotional resilience in children.

Techniques for Breathing and Relaxation

Stress management can also benefit from breathing exercises and relaxation methods. You can teach your child these strategies to help them relax their thoughts, alleviate physical stress, and slow their breathing. By incorporating these techniques into your daily routine, you can also maintain your composure under pressure.

Decide a Specific Time to Let Go of All Your Concerns

Give your child a specific 30-minute window each day to voice all of their worries to help them minimise the amount of time they spend worrying. Rather than letting them worry throughout the day, setting aside the same time each day can help guarantee that they have a safe place and time to do so.

Make Dua

> *The Prophet Muhammad (PBUH) used to make a dua seeking refuge from worry, saying, "Oh Allah! I seek refuge in You from worry and sadness, from weakness and laziness, from miserliness and cowardice, from being overcome by debt and from being overpowered by men" (Sahih Bukhari)*

Allah (SWT) desires us to invoke Him. By converting your worries and anxieties into regular prayers for your child's anxiousness, you can teach them to turn to Allah (SWT) when needed.

Managing stress and mental health from an Islamic perspective involves recognising symptoms, providing timely support, and implementing spiritual and practical coping strategies. Islam emphasises patience, trust in Allah, prayer, and acts of kindness as essential for achieving mental well-being. The Quran and Hadith provide profound wisdom on handling stress, reminding believers that hardships are temporary and that with hardship come ease as the Quran states:

> *"For indeed, with hardship comes ease. Indeed, with hardship comes ease" (Quran 94:5-6)*

By integrating Islamic teachings into daily life, individuals can develop resilience, maintain mental well-being, and navigate challenges with faith and confidence.

Chapter Eleven

Role of Parents & Community in Supporting Children's Development

Parental Role in Child Development

Islam emphasises the immense responsibility of parents in shaping their children's character, values, and emotional resilience. Effective parenting requires a balance of love, discipline, and guidance rooted in faith and wisdom.

Responsibilities of Parents in Shaping Their Children's Mental and Emotional Health

A child's first school is their home, and parents are their primary teachers. Providing a stable and nurturing environment is essential in fostering confidence and emotional security. A home filled with love, support, and guidance lays the foundation for a child's growth and well-being. When children feel safe and valued, they develop a strong sense of self and are more likely to navigate life's challenges with resilience.

Teaching self-awareness and emotional intelligence is crucial in helping children recognise and manage their emotions. Encouraging them to develop patience and self-control strengthens their character and decision-making abilities.

> *"And those who restrain anger and pardon the people—Allah loves the doers of good." (Quran 3:134)*

By nurturing emotional intelligence, parents equip their children to handle conflicts calmly and make choices that align with Islamic values.

Instilling a growth mindset ensures that children embrace learning and self-improvement with perseverance and a positive attitude. Parents should encourage problem-solving and resilience rather than a fear of failure. When children understand that effort and persistence lead to success, they become more motivated to overcome obstacles and continue striving for excellence in their education and personal development.

Promoting positive social interaction is vital in shaping a child's ability to build meaningful relationships. Teaching respect, empathy, and kindness allows them to navigate social situations with understanding and sincerity.

> *"The best among you are those who have the best manners and character" (Sahih Bukhari)*

Parents should model these qualities in their interactions, demonstrating how good character strengthens faith and community bonds.

Encouraging open and honest discussions fosters trust and communication between parents and children. When children feel comfortable expressing their thoughts and concerns, they're more likely to seek guidance without fear of judgment.

Parents should remain approachable and provide solutions rooted in Islamic principles, ensuring their children grow up with a strong moral compass and the confidence to make righteous decisions in life.

Engaging in Self-Improvement and Education as a Model for Children

Children mirror their parents' habits and behaviours, making it essential for parents to prioritise their personal growth. By investing in self-improvement—whether through reading, learning new skills, or deepening their understanding of Islam—parents set a strong example for their children.

When children observe their parents striving for knowledge and self-betterment, they naturally develop a mindset that values continuous learning and self-discipline.

Parenting requires patience and wisdom, qualities that Islam strongly encourages. Handling challenges with composure and thoughtfulness teaches children to navigate difficulties with a calm and measured approach.

> *"Indeed, Allah is with the patient." (Quran 2:153)*

When parents demonstrate patience in their words and actions, they create a home environment where children feel secure, understood, and encouraged to practice emotional self-control.

Fostering a spirit of lifelong learning begins with parents showing enthusiasm for religious and worldly knowledge. When children see their parents eager to explore new ideas, engage in discussions, and seek wisdom, they develop a natural curiosity and love for learning. Encouraging intellectual growth not only broadens a child's understanding of the world but also strengthens their connection to faith, reinforcing the importance of seeking knowledge as a lifelong pursuit.

Community Support and Resources

Raising a child requires support beyond the immediate family. A strong, faith-centered community provides additional guidance, encouragement, and a sense of belonging.

Utilising Community Resources and Support Networks for Parenting Assistance

Raising children in accordance with Islamic teachings requires patience, wisdom, and knowledge. Parents must seek guidance from Islamic scholars and experienced mentors to navigate the complexities of parenting while upholding Islam's values. Scholars provide insights rooted in the Qur'an and Sunnah, ensuring that parents make informed decisions in line with Allah's (SWT) teachings.

Consulting knowledgeable individuals within the community allows parents to receive well-rounded advice on discipline, character development, and instilling faith in their children. Their wisdom helps address modern challenges while staying true to Islamic principles, allowing families to raise children who embody strong moral values and a deep connection to their faith.

Islamic centres and mosques are essential in providing parenting and mental health resources. These institutions often offer educational programs, workshops, support groups, and counselling services tailored to address parenting challenges and child development. Mental well-being is a crucial aspect of raising emotionally strong and resilient children.

Seeking professional guidance within an Islamic framework helps parents manage stress, discipline compassionately, and create a nurturing family environment. A balanced approach integrating Islamic teachings with psychological well-being allows parents to support their children's emotional, spiritual, and intellectual growth. Parents can cultivate a loving and supportive household that reinforces faith and positive character by understanding their children's unique needs and challenges.

Parenting can be overwhelming at times, but building a network of like-minded parents offers encouragement and support. Connecting with other Muslim parents fosters a sense of community where experiences, challenges, and advice can be shared. This collective approach strengthens individual parenting skills while reinforcing Islamic values within families.

When parents come together to discuss concerns, participate in group activities, and engage in shared learning, they create a strong foundation for their children's moral and spiritual upbringing. A community-oriented approach to parenting ensures that children grow up in an environment that nurtures their faith, character, and social development.

Parents can navigate the challenges of raising children by fostering a supportive network, seeking guidance from knowledgeable sources, and remaining committed to Islamic values. The journey of parenting is filled with learning opportunities, and relying on both religious wisdom and psychological understanding helps raise confident, responsible, and faith-driven individuals.

With a strong foundation in Islamic teachings and practical strategies for mental and emotional well-being, parents can nurture children who practice their faith and contribute positively to society. Through patience, shared learning, and reliance on the teachings of Islam, parents can fulfil their responsibility of raising righteous and compassionate children, ensuring that they uphold the values of Islam throughout their lives.

Encouraging Involvement in Islamic Community Activities to Foster Growth and Support

Instilling Islamic values in children requires more than verbal instruction; it demands practical experiences that reinforce morality and faith. Community events such as Quran recitation circles, charity drives, and cultural programs offer children opportunities to see Islamic teachings in action. These activities help them internalise the principles of compassion, generosity, and honesty, fostering a deep connection to their faith. By actively participating in such gatherings, children learn that Islam (SWT) is a way of life that extends beyond personal worship into their interactions with the community.

Encouraging children to participate in organising community initiatives fosters a sense of leadership and responsibility. Whether helping to plan an event at the mosque, leading a small project, or assisting younger peers, these experiences build confidence and accountability. Through such involvement, children develop essential skills like teamwork, problem-solving, and decision-making, all within an Islamic framework. By entrusting them with meaningful roles, parents and mentors instil a sense of purpose and belonging, preparing them to be proactive members of the Ummah.

Islam teaches the importance of giving back, and parents play a vital role in nurturing this value. Encouraging children to engage in acts of charity—whether through donating, volunteering at food drives, or assisting neighbours—instils humility and gratitude. Through service, children recognise the blessings Allah (SWT) has granted them and develop empathy for those in need. This mindset strengthens their faith and helps them grow into compassionate individuals who contribute positively to society.

A strong connection to faith begins with a solid foundation in Islamic knowledge. Enrolling children in Islamic schools, weekend madrasahs, and youth programs ensures they understand their religious and cultural heritage. Exposure to Islamic teachings in a structured setting helps children develop a deep love for their faith, equipping them with the knowledge and confidence to uphold their identity in diverse environments.

Parents and communities must work hand in hand to provide children with the guidance, education, and support necessary for their holistic development. A child raised with love, faith, and a sense of responsibility will grow into one who contributes positively to society.

> *The Prophet Muhammad (PBUH) stated: "The most beloved of people to Allah is the one who brings the most benefit to others" (Al-Mujam al-Awsat)*

Through intentional parenting and active community participation, we can nurture a generation that upholds Islamic values and strives for excellence in all aspects of life.

Chapter Twelve

Conclusion

Parenting is a journey filled with countless moments of joy, learning, and challenges. As Muslim parents, our responsibility extends beyond simply raising children; we're entrusted with nurturing their faith, shaping their character, and equipping them with the emotional and mental strength to navigate life successfully. Through the teachings of Islam, we're blessed with a divine guide to parenting—one that emphasises love, compassion, wisdom, and patience.

Throughout this book, we have explored key strategies rooted in Islamic principles that support the holistic development of children. We have delved into the importance of faith as the foundation of a child's identity, the role of emotional intelligence in fostering resilience, and the power of effective communication in building trust. We have also examined how discipline, self-esteem, gratitude, and social skills contribute to a child's well-being and how parents can create a nurturing environment that supports their mental and emotional health. As we conclude, reflecting on the overarching themes will serve as a lifelong guide for raising strong, balanced, and faithful children is crucial.

Faith is the bedrock upon which a child's moral compass and worldview are built. By instilling strong Islamic beliefs and values from an early age, we give our children an anchor that will keep them grounded throughout life's trials and tribulations. Teaching them about Tawhid (oneness of Allah (SWT)), the importance of Salah, and the beauty of good character based on the Sunnah of the Prophet Muhammad (PBUH) will help them develop a deep connection with their Creator.

A child who grows up knowing Allah (SWT) is their ultimate protector, guide, and source of strength will be more resilient in facing difficulties. As parents, our role is to continuously reinforce this faith by practising what we preach, being role models in our daily lives, and integrating Islamic teachings into everyday experiences. Through consistency in worship and open discussions about Islam, we ensure that faith becomes a natural and cherished part of their identity.

Raising emotionally intelligent children is essential in today's complex world. Emotional intelligence allows children to recognise and manage emotions, empathise with others, and handle interpersonal relationships wisely. Islam encourages self-awareness, patience, and emotional regulation, all crucial for mental well-being. Teaching children how to process their feelings, express themselves appropriately, and seek solace in prayer and dua fosters resilience.

Resilience is the ability to bounce back from setbacks and challenges. As parents, we must teach our children that hardships are a part of life but that they can overcome any obstacle with faith and perseverance. The stories of the Prophets serve as powerful lessons in resilience—whether it's Prophet Yusuf's patience in the face of betrayal, Prophet Ayub's endurance through illness, or Prophet Musa's trust in Allah (SWT) while facing adversity. By sharing these stories and emphasising reliance on Allah (SWT), children learn that trials are temporary and their strength comes from their faith and inner resolve.

Effective communication strengthens the parent-child relationship and fosters a sense of security and trust. Children thrive in environments where they feel heard, valued, and respected. The Prophet Muhammad (PBUH) exemplified the best communication practices—he listened attentively, spoke with kindness, and always encouraged dialogue.

Creating open lines of communication with children allows them to share their thoughts, fears, and aspirations without hesitation. As parents, we should strive to be approachable and non-judgmental, using active listening and positive reinforcement to guide our children. Encouraging our children to express themselves freely and validating their emotions will not only enhance their confidence but also prevent feelings of isolation and misunderstanding.

Islamic discipline is centred on love, fairness, and wisdom. It's not about punishment but teaching accountability and guiding our children toward righteous behaviour. The Prophet was never harsh with children; instead, he corrected mistakes with patience and gentleness.

Discipline should be rooted in understanding, clear expectations, and consistency. Harsh punishment can lead to fear rather than learning, whereas compassionate and constructive discipline fosters self-discipline and responsibility. Teaching our children the concept of consequences in a way that aligns with Islamic ethics will help them develop a strong moral compass and an innate sense of right and wrong.

A child's self-worth is greatly influenced by their upbringing. Encouraging self-confidence and self-esteem is vital for their success and well-being. Islam teaches us that every individual is created with purpose and dignity. When children recognise their unique strengths and abilities, they develop a positive self-image and the courage to pursue their dreams.

As parents, we play a significant role in nurturing confidence by affirming our children's abilities, celebrating their achievements (big or small), and allowing them to take on challenges with encouragement. Providing opportunities for independence and decision-making will empower children to believe in themselves. Most importantly, instilling the belief that their worth is not defined by societal standards but by their character and relationship with Allah (SWT) will safeguard them from insecurity and external pressures.

In a world driven by materialism and competition, teaching children gratitude and contentment is a priceless gift. Islam reminds us to appreciate what we have rather than constantly seeking what we lack. When children learn to be grateful, they develop a sense of inner peace and happiness that is not dependent on external factors.

As parents, we can encourage gratitude by modelling it in our own lives, incorporating daily reflection, and reminding children of Allah's (SWT) blessings. Teaching our children to say Alhamdulillah in all situations and to focus on the positives rather than dwelling on what they do not have fosters a mindset of contentment and humility.

Raising children is not solely the responsibility of parents; it's a collective effort that involves the wider community. A strong support system—including extended family, teachers, mentors, and peers—plays a crucial role in a child's development. The Prophet (PBUH) emphasised the importance of the ummah (community) and encouraged mutual care and guidance. Surrounding children with positive role models and an environment reinforcing Islamic values will strengthen their moral foundation. Encouraging participation in community activities, Islamic studies, and social engagements will also help them build meaningful connections and develop a strong sense of belonging.

Raising mentally strong and emotionally balanced children in today's world is a challenging yet deeply rewarding endeavour. By anchoring our parenting in Islamic principles, we give our children the tools they need to thrive in this life and the Hereafter. Faith, emotional intelligence, communication, discipline, confidence, gratitude, and community are the pillars that will support their growth and well-being.

As parents, our ultimate goal is to raise children who love and obey Allah (SWT), are kind and just, contribute positively to society, and remain steadfast in their faith despite life's trials. The effort we put into their upbringing today will shape their future and the generations to come. May Allah (SWT) guide us as parents, grant us wisdom and patience, and bless our children with righteousness, strength, and unwavering faith. Ameen.

Find Out More

Website: www.barakahinbusiness.com

Socials: @barakahinbusiness

If you enjoyed this book, kindly leave a review to help expand our reach so others may benefit also.

www.ingramcontent.com/pod-product-compliance
Lightning Source LLC
Chambersburg PA
CBHW071213070526
44584CB00019B/3019